HENRY MILLER:
THREE DECADES OF CRITICISM

HENRY MILLER:
THREE DECADES
OF CRITICISM

Edited and with an Introduction by
Edward Mitchell

New York University Press
New York   1971

ACKNOWLEDGMENTS

From "Inside the Whale" in SUCH, SUCH WERE THE JOYS, by George Orwell, copyright 1945, 1952, 1953, by Sonia Brownell Orwell. Reprinted by permission of Harcourt, Brace & World, Inc., Martin Secker & Warburg, Ltd., and Miss Sonia Brownell.

"Henry Miller" in *Image and Idea,* by Philip Rahv, copyright 1949 by Philip Rahv. Reprinted by permission of Philip Rahv.

"Shadow of Doom: An Essay on Henry Miller," by Wallace Fowlie. Reprinted from *Accent,* Autumn, 1944, by permission of Wallace Fowlie.

From "Further Interpretations" in *Freudianism and the Literary Mind,* by Frederick J. Hoffman, copyright 1945 by Louisiana State University Press. Reprinted by permission of Louisiana State University Press.

"Death and the Baroque," by Aldous Huxley, copyright 1949 by Aldous Huxley. Reprinted by permission of Mrs. Aldous Huxley.

"Henry Miller—The Pathology of Isolation," by Alwyn Lee, copyright 1952 by Alwyn Lee. Reprinted by permission of Alwyn Lee.

From "The Greatest Living Author," by Karl Shapiro, copyright 1959 by Karl Shapiro. Reprinted from IN DEFENSE OF IGNORANCE, by Karl Shapiro, by permission of Random House, Inc.

From "Henry Miller and John Betjeman" in PUZZLES AND EPIPH-ANIES, by Frank Kermode. Copyright 1962 by Frank Kermode. Reprinted by permission of Chilmark Press and Routledge & Kegan Paul, Ltd.

"The Tropics of Miller," by David Littlejohn, copyright 1962 by *The New Republic.* Reprinted by permission of *The New Republic,* Harrison-Blaine of New Jersey, Inc.

"The Legacy of Henry Miller" in HENRY MILLER, by Kingsley Widmer, copyright 1963 by Twayne Publishers, Inc. Reprinted by permission of Twayne Publishers, Inc.

From "Alienation and Rebellion to Nowhere" in EXISTENTIALISM

CONTENTS

BIOGRAPHY

1891   Henry Valentine Miller born December 26 in New York City of lower middleclass German-American family.

1892   Moved to Williamsburg section of Brooklyn. This childhood home contributed the materials for the famous "14th Ward" and other recollections of early years.

1909   Formal education terminated when Miller dropped out of classes at City College of New York.

1910–13   Employed in shortlived clerical jobs. Traveled to the West Coast and met Emma Goldman in San Diego.

1914   Returned to New York and worked with father in tailor shop.

1917–19   Married Beatrice S. Wickens of Brooklyn, a pianist. Daughter Barbara born. Employed in various jobs including U. S. Bureau of Economic Research.

1920   Employed as messenger then as employment manager for Western Union Telegraph Company of New York.

1922   Wrote first, unsuccessful, novel (*Clipped Wings*) during three weeks vacation from Western Union.

1924   Left Western Union, divorced first wife and married June Edith Smith, the Mona/Mara prototype of his later novels.

1925–27   Opened a speakeasy with wife June, sold his own "mezotints" door to door, was salesman, clerk and occasional beggar. Compiled notes for complete "autobiographical" cycle of novels.

1928   Toured Europe with June on money donated by her friend.

1929   Returned to New York where novel *This Gentile World* was completed. This work was never published.

1930–31   Returned to Europe without wife or income. Met Anaïs Nin in Louveciennes. Began writing *Tropic of Cancer* while living a day to day existence. Worked as proofreader on the Paris edition of Chicago Tribune. Taught English at Dijon during winter.

1933   Lived in Clichy with Alfred Perles. Wrote *Black Spring*.

1934   Came to Number 18 Villa Seurat. *Tropic of Cancer* published. Frequent arguments with Lowenfels and Fraenkel on the death theme. Visited New York. Divorced from June by proxy in Mexico City.

1935–36   *Aller Retour New York* published. Began *Hamlet* correspondence with Michael Fraenkel. Visited New York a second time.

1937   Met Lawrence Durrell. Began publication of *The Booster* and *Delta* with Alfred Perles.

1938   Publication of *Money and How It Gets That Way* and *Max And The White Phagocytes* (later titled *The Cosmological Eye*).

1939   *Tropic of Capricorn* published. Visited Lawrence Durrell in Greece. Met George Katsimbalis (the Colossus). Source of regular income closed with death of Paris publisher, Jack Kahane and the demise of the Obelisk Press shortly after beginning of the Second World War.

1940   Because of the outbreak of war returned to New York. Visited home of Caresse Crosby. Wrote *The Colossus of Maroussi, The World of Sex, Quiet Days in Clichy* and began *Sexus*.

1941   Made automobile tour of the United States accompanied part of the way by painter Abraham Rattner.

1942–44   Settled in Los Angeles. Wrote numerous essays and reviews and began serious work in watercolors. Numerous watercolor exhibitions during this period. Married third wife, Martha Lepska.

1945   Daughter Valentine born. Completed *Sexus* and *Air Conditioned Nightmare*. Made home in Big Sur, California.

1946–47   Second volume of American sketches, *Remember to Remember*, finished. Further exhibitions of water colors.

1948   Son Tony born. Visit of astrologer and friend Moricand later written up under title of *A Devil In Paradise*.

1949   *Sexus* published.

1952–53   Divorced from third wife. Wrote *The Books In My Life*. Returned to Europe for half-year tour. Married Eve McClure. *Plexus* published.

1954–57   *Time of the Assassins* published. Also *Big Sur and the Oranges of Hieronymous Bosch*. Constant stream of visitors and friends to Big Sur home.

1959–60   Publication of *Nexus* and *To Paint Is To Love Again*.

1961   Separated from fourth wife. Beginning of frequent return trips to Europe. *Tropic of Cancer* first published in the United States, subject of numerous court cases for censorship.

1962–63   Undertook considerable travel at home and abroad. First American edition of *Tropic of Capricorn*. Publication of first play, *Just Wild About Harry,* and collection of occasional pieces, *Stand Still Like The Hummingbird.*

1964–69   American publication of all Miller's works including *The World of Sex* and *Sexus, Plexus* and *Nexus*. Married to Hoki Hiroko Tokuda in 1967. Record of courtship of Miss Tokuda published as *Insomnia: or The Devil At Large.*

INTRODUCTION

It is a fitting historical coincidence that the assessments of Henry Miller's work represented in this volume should begin with the issues first joined by George Orwell and close with the invaluable perspective offered by William Gordon. It seems to me that it is the polarity so brilliantly represented by these selections which has in other cases, often unconsciously, caused many of the people who have written about Henry Miller to be seriously handicapped by partisanship in one form or another. Partly by way of offering a rationale for this collection of essays, I propose briefly to consider the two basic orientations from which Miller's work has usually been judged, for I believe that what this collection of essays reveals is that the two are often illuminatingly complementary.

It was 1930 when Miller disembarked for his second, this time sustained, immersion in the particular current and temper of European life which nourished him. The psychological and symbolic significance of that emigration is recorded in the third volume of *The Rosy Crucifixion,* but nothing which was to come from Miller's pen in the next twenty years would suggest any particular cognizance of the fact that this voyage was preceded, only months before, by the worst economic and social crisis his homeland was to know, or that his arrival in France was followed by one of the most disruptive decades in European history. If Miller turns his attention to matters economic, it is to consider the cosmically hilarious aspects of "Money And How It Gets That Way." When he returned to America in the winter of 1934 for the first of two brief visits, he found his native land to be still the epitome of the chromium-plated, neon-illuminated, cellophane-wrapped existence he had written about in "Aller Retour New York." Neither of these pieces has much artistic merit. Indeed, one is little more than a *jeu d'esprit*. Nor are they important to the body of Miller's work except perhaps as manifestations of a basic attitude which has remained virtually unchanged for thirty-five years. Their real significance lies in the recognition that, had they ever been broadly disseminated among the audience in relation to which they were written, they would likely have met with a very indifferent, if not openly hostile, reception.

It is this fact which goes far to explain the more significant lack of general response to *The Tropic of Cancer* (1934). That Lawrence Durrell was one of the few to have *Tropic of Cancer* burst upon him like a bomb can only partially be attributed to the modest first edition and the subsequent irony of its appeal to the "pornographic" market. That the novel had gone through five authorized and at least two pirated editions by 1939 is evidence of a not inconsiderable distribution. And those who, like George Orwell, took issue with Miller's socio-political obliviousness still acknowledged that the novel manifested a vitality, an audacious artistic integrity, that marked a work of significance. The *literati* in America, and in Europe also, were not so much unprepared for, as simply uncongenial toward, Miller's work. The heyday of American literary expatriotism had long since passed. And the work of the Surrealists and Dadaists, from which Miller was at first thought to be descended, seemed hopelessly trivial and irrelevant to critics, writers, and readers who were at that moment sharing, perhaps for the first time in America, an overwhelming sense of economic collapse, social injustice, and political betrayal. A few of the significant literary events that took place in America in the years between 1930 and 1939 suggest the taste and temper which prevailed during the period. These years saw the publication of Mary Heaton Vorse's *Strike* (1930), Richard Wright's

Uncle Tom's Children (1936) and John Steinbeck's *Grapes of Wrath* (1939). What Edmund Wilson called "the class war" in literature was opened by Michael Gold's scathing attack on Thornton Wilder as a "genteel Christ" in *The New Republic* for October 1930. Granville Hicks' *The Great Tradition,* a Marxist approach to American literature since the Civil War, was published in 1935, the year of the First American Writers Congress. Nothing could be more characteristic of this era than its impatience with, or more often willing ignorance of, an unknown American earthly expressing the cosmic joyousness of the marginal life in Paris.

Yet it would be a mistake to conclude from all this that Henry Miller is not a man of his times, which is to say a writer of the twenties and thirties. It is sometimes forgotten that the fictional incidents in *The Rosy Crucifixion* cover only one decade and that the materials forming the whole of the "autobiographical" novels cover less than two decades. And these decades are, as Miller has repeatedly insisted, very much those of a Brooklyn boy. Apart from *The Tropic of Cancer,* which is only fully intelligible as the experience of an American, and *Quiet Days in Clichy,* which is a less successful coda to the earlier novel, the remainder of Miller's autobiographical fiction deals with what is unmistakably an urban American experience. Because *Tropic of Cancer* is the last in the fictional sequence of the five "autobiographical" novels, and therefore deals with the consequences of a pilgrimage which is virtually complete, it is to the *Tropic of Capricorn,* and the three novels comprising *The Rosy Crucifixion* that we must look for materials which are indigenous to Henry Miller, both as artist and persona.

Henry Miller's principal source for materials is, of course, the city itself. For Miller, one of the chief examples of the nightmare world of metropolitan New York is the "Cosmodeamonic Telegraph Company of North America." Western Union, as Miller portrays it in *Tropic of Capricorn,* is clearly a microcosm of the social heartlessness and economic brutality which, like so many of his contemporaries, Miller found to be characteristic of the whole of American society. However, his first novel, which drew directly upon his experience as personnel manager for Western Union, and in which he undertook to sabotage the Horatio Alger myth by treating in documentary fashion the actual lives of twelve men whom he had known as messenger boys, was a colossal failure. As Miller recounts it in *Tropic of Capricorn,* this first novel collapsed under the weight of its author's commitment to "the facts." The difference between the earlier abortive novel and the later works is that Western Union as a sordid example of social and economic fact is, in *Capricorn,* entirely at the service of the "cosmodeamonic" as an ontological symbol. Miller still presents the facts, in abundance, but their relevance has been radically altered. Indeed, the facts have relevance only as they relate to the spiritual maturation of the protagonist who is only at the beginning of his journey in *Tropic of Capricorn.* Consequently, there is a double irony in the narrator's repeated insistence that many of the facts of his existence—the managerial insanity of Western Union, the aimless wandering through city streets, the casual if violent sexual encounters—are "without meaning." Not only are they meaningless because the individual human cannot extract order from them, but they are also meaningless until they are viewed as the appropriate but nevertheless accidental conditions of a "rebirth" which, in itself, is considered the only important event in human existence.

It is chiefly for this reason that it is impossible to place Miller in the company of those writers of the thirties and forties whom we ordinarily think of in terms of "social protest." As George Orwell early pointed out and as other commentators have often repeated, Miller lacks the fundamental commitment to the existential particularities of a regional, social, and political environment which characterizes literature of social protest. It is fundamentally a question of means and end. The evils of social injustice, environmental stultification, and even the erosion of basic morality from which they stem, is an occasion for sustained outrage only if the human being is seen as defining himself by means of interaction with an immediate and significantly individual context. Outrage, a desire for remedial action, or even admiration for human virtues in the face of overwhelmingly inimical odds is a relevant response if the individual is viewed in relation to an environment which forms him and to which he may effectively contribute. But to place the social and material environment beneath a character's concern, which is the ultimate product of the liberation which Miller's persona achieves, has the same effect as placing it beyond his control. In both cases any remedial action aimed at effecting social justice is inconceivable.

The point here is an important one because it sheds light on Miller's persistent modernity as well as his integral relation to a perennial strain of the American temper. The crux of the matter lies in the fundamental difference between Miller's work and that mode of modern literature which is also radically ontological— French existentialism. The existential position is characterized by the view that the universe is indifferent or possibly even inimical to man. Man's existence therefore is one of necessary cosmological alienation—it is a given of the human condition. Miller, in contrast, finds that reality is indifferent to man only in so far as reality is a process which executes its own laws with or without man's awareness of it. While Miller would agree that man is at present alienated from reality, he repudiates the premise that cosmological alienation is a necessary condition of man's existence. Man's alienation is human rather than cosmological because it is a condition for which man, not the structure of the universe, is responsible. Because Miller finds that alienation belies the integral connection which he takes to exist between man and reality-as-process, he insists that no orientation toward life is workable which accepts alienation as a norm.

Consequently, man's alienation, although it may be widespread, is individual rather than cosmological. As a result, Miller stands apart from the existentialists because the self, the awakening of which his fictional odyssey portrays, is finally an essence— a consistent capacity discoverable in a relationship—rather than, as the self is for Sartre, an unavoidably incomplete entity to be created. Moreover, he is differentiated from the realists and naturalists in that the concrete particulars in his novels are graphic but not discreet, they are illustrative without being formative. It is impossible to envision Miller's persona as "the product of" or "victimized by" any society in a collective or institutional sense.

His environment is, if you will, accidental. Consequently he cannot be representative of anything less than mankind considered in the abstract.

The temptation to view Miller as one who wilfully refuses to acknowledge the consequences of the social and cultural horrors which he portrays so graphically results from the failure to take into account, or perhaps the inability to accept, the syncretism which issues from the ontology which Miller shares with other American transcendentalists. However, to approach Miller as an abstracted apotheosis, a literary guru, ignores not only his craft as an artist, but the more fundamental fact that the incidents in his novels, the experiences his persona undergoes, even if they were utterly fortuitous, are still contiguous: They transpire in some relation to something. And that something is composed of materials which are very much urban, American, and twentieth century and that, although it may serve largely the function of an analogue, still has resonances and overtones not shared by, say, Walden Pond.

In a somewhat broader perspective of American literature, perhaps Henry Miller could well be seen as standing somewhere in the midst of the unlikely triangle formed by Walt Whitman, Christopher Newman, and Jimmy Herf. The experience and much of the reaction of Miller's persona is that of Herf. Miller's hero, however, comes to discover just how far "pretty far" actually is. The innocence which Miller's "I" carries to Europe proves to be the source of his strength rather than, as in Newman's case, his weakness. If Newman is defeated by the very characteristics which make him *the* American, Miller's persona finds it possible to succeed by transmogrifying those characteristics, thereby once again reifying that elusive but perennial abstraction which Whitman had earlier called "the procreant urge of the world."

HENRY MILLER:
THREE DECADES OF CRITICISM

The Forties

It is difficult to summarize so insightful and far ranging an essay as that written by George Orwell on Henry Miller's work. He immediately perceived, for example, the crucial distinction between *Tropic of Cancer* and such works as *Ulysses* and *Voyage to the Bottom of Night*. He was also among the earliest to point out Miller's efforts to reproduce throughout his narration the syntax and rhythms of the spoken language rather than to use the rhetorical devices of the interior monologue. But the most revelatory sections of Orwell's essay are found chiefly in his comments on the similarities between Miller and Whitman. Orwell's view of Whitman's America seems somewhat naïve today. He dismisses Whitman's candid appraisal of America and his warnings regarding its future in *Democratic Vistas*. And Orwell's willingness to believe in the virtually unlimited possibilities of nineteenth-century America is now impossible to share. But all that is largely beside the point. What matters is the commitments which underlie the comments. And Orwell, despite his apparent pessimism, clearly is committed to notions of change, if not of progress, and to man's contribution to, and thus at least partial responsibility for, his sociopolitical environment.

On the surface, it appears that Orwell objects most strenuously to Miller's indiscriminate "acceptance" of the whole twentieth century, an acceptance which then includes "concentration camps, rubber truncheons, Hitler, Stalin, bombs," and much, much more. In fact, however, what Orwell actually finds objectionable in Miller is the position of acceptance per se because acceptance is passive and entails an indifference to the whole of one's environment. The question Orwell is asking is whether, at the time of the outbreak of World War II, indifference is defensible. While such a question is hardly original, Orwell's response to it may be. On the one hand, given "the break-up of laissez-faire capitalism and of the liberal-Christian culture," Orwell finds that Miller's passivity and indifference may be the only justifiable literary stance. On the other hand, it is only "as a writer" that Miller is precluded from playing an effective role in the world's affairs, implying that perhaps all writers, Miller included, would be well advised to engage in some other, more effective activity.

Considerable argument has been raised against the point of view from which Orwell views Miller. But rather than attempt to decide the issue or pass judgment on either bias, the wiser course is perhaps to acknowledge that the quarrel, if that is what it is, is "perennial," as Aldous Huxley, in another context, has called it.

Philip Rahv's essay is noteworthy on several counts. It was one of the first to call attention to the need for drawing a distinction between merely exploiting one's personality and the more general necessity of exploiting any material for artistic purpose. The failure to draw such distinctions leads, particularly in the case of a writer like Miller, to critical partisanship. More importantly, it frustrates a comprehension of the "biographical" as a narrative strategy. While it would probably no longer be possible to agree that the ego of Miller's persona is "confused and helpless" in the face of exterior reality, there is no doubt that Miller was and is of the opinion that man can no longer afford the continual sacrifice of personality required by creative acts of the kind represented by Joyce and Proust. Perhaps the most disputable of Rahv's contentions is that Miller is "nihilistic" in his subversion of certain values. It seems particularly strange today to view Miller as negating Whitman's affirmation of self and life. But we need to recall that this judgment lacks the perspective offered by the subsequent publication of *Sexus, Plexus,* and *Nexus.* Whatever distortion the unavoidable lack of such a perspective may have caused, Rahv clearly saw that rather than belonging with that growing number of moderns whose alienation threw them back on "narcissistic attitudes," Miller "accepted his alienated status" and, indeed, found within it the sign of his salvation.

Not the least provocative aspect of Wallace Fowlie's essay is his contention that Miller has "interrupted the traditional American treatment of evil," which is another way of acknowledging that there is a large and not always easily divided stream in American literature one branch of which is perhaps best represented by Melville, the other by Whitman. However, the principal subject of "Shadow of Doom" is the role of the artist in the modern world. While Fowlie shares the view that modern life presents itself to man as particularly dislocated and atomized, he differs from Rahv and Hoffman in that he takes the view that modern life should not tempt us into artistic self-dissolution, but rather that modern life should oblige us to organize the chaos of experience into coherent patterns. Fowlie locates Miller's literary heritage in the work of Rimbaud, thereby offering some literary context for such terms as "prophet" and "seer" as these are applied to Miller. The modern artist is captured particularly well by Miller in the projection of the artist-hero who is "the little man who is terrified and who in reality is greater than that which terrifies him." But despite his role as rediscoverer and indemnifier of the significance of human existence, there is, as Fowlie only partially acknowledges, something confining and narrow in the concept of the artist as visionary. Perhaps because the "love of the visionary is his vision" the effect which the visionary as artist produces is the indifference and lack of involvement which Orwell comments upon.

Frederick Hoffman was one of the first to explore in any detail the Freudian implications in Miller's work. Particularly, Hoffman calls attention to the relation between the nonrational, nonlogical aspects of man's experience as Miller and others portray them and the functioning of the preconscious and unconscious as Freudian theory deduces it. The value of the nonrational lies in its positive correction of the "Hamlet disease"—the compulsive effort to find a rationally satisfactory justification of man's personal and collective existence. Hoffman also distinguishes between Miller's happy acceptance of "the new opportunity which psychoanalysis affords of viewing a world previously shut off from consciousness" and Miller's rejection of the uses to which psychoanalysis, as a clinical practice, has been put. Interestingly, however, Hoffman barely alludes to the fact that Miller's antipathy to Freudianism is theoretical as well as clinical. Guilt, for Miller, is the result of an error, the compulsion to achieve an individually derived, rational indemnification for one's existence. For Miller the correction for such error is relatively simple. When we cease to make certain demands, the cessation on the part of the universe or on the part of humanity to comply with those demands is no longer a matter even of concern, let alone guilt. For Freud, however, guilt was not ancillary but radical. It is a given of the civilized, which is to say human, condition. *Civilization And Its Discontents* is a study of how and why mankind cannot escape guilt. Whatever is to be said on this score, Hoffman was almost clairvoyant in his prediction that Miller's early, almost biological, resignation might well issue in "a religious-aesthetic view of the universe." And his description of Miller's notion of peace as "achieved by a passive dwelling within the grotesque and obscene chaos of the world's unconscious being" is sufficiently different from William Gordon's conclusions to repay careful comparison.

"Death And The Baroque" is unique in this collection in that it is the only essay which is not, strictly speaking, a work of literary criticism. The references to Miller's work, in fact to any work of literature, are oblique and brief. Even the Baroque tombs are not the subject of Huxley's essay. He is interested in an artistic impulse, a particular but constant aspect of the human condition rendered in art, which any art at any time can reflect and for which the Baroque period is particularly known.

Huxley's is one of the few essays which links Miller's work with something more than a narrowly literary cult or *ism*. In other words, it offers a truly comparative base in the arts from which Miller's work might be viewed. As others had already noticed, there is something Gargantuan, something bordering upon caricature, in Miller's art. The value of Huxley's essay is that it offers a wider perspective from which the "art of the inordinate" can be viewed. If Huxley is correct in his contention that those experiences which are inescapably, inviolably private—death, sex, the mystical—are also unavoidably nonpublic, unsocial, ahistorical, then we may have a more adequate explanation than "pornography" for the ambivalence and discomfort which Miller's work seems so often to arouse.

INSIDE THE WHALE

George Orwell

When *Tropic of Cancer* was published the Italians were marching into Abyssinia and Hitler's concentration-camps were already bulging. The intellectual foci of the world were Rome, Moscow, and Berlin. It did not seem to be a moment at which a novel of understanding value was likely to be written about American dead-beats cadging drinks in the Latin Quarter. Of course a novelist is not obliged to write directly about contemporary history, but a novelist who simply disregards the major public events of the moment is generally either a footler or a plain idiot. From a mere account of the subject matter of *Tropic of Cancer* most people would probably assume it to be no more than a bit of naughty-naughty left over from the 'twenties. Actually, nearly everyone who read it saw at once that it was nothing of the kind, but a very remarkable book. How or why remarkable? That question is never easy to answer. It is better to begin by describing the impression that *Tropic of Cancer* has left on my own mind.

When I first opened *Tropic of Cancer* and saw that it was full of unprintable words, my immediate reaction was a refusal to be impressed. Most people's would be the same, I believe. Nevertheless, after a lapse of time the atmosphere of the book, besides innumerable details, seemed to linger in my memory in a peculiar way. A year later Miller's second book, *Black Spring,* was published. By this time *Tropic of Cancer* was much more vividly present in my mind than it had been when I first read it. My first feeling about *Black Spring* was that it showed a falling-off, and it is a fact that it has not the same unity as the other book. Yet after another year there were many passages in *Black Spring* that had also rooted themselves in my memory. Evidently these books are of the sort to leave a flavour behind them—books that "create a world of their own," as the saying goes. The books that do this are not necessarily good books, they may be good bad books like *Raffles* or the *Sherlock Holmes* stories, or perverse and morbid books like *Wuthering Heights* or *The House with the Green Shutters.* But now and again there appears a novel which opens up a new world not by revealing what is strange, but by revealing what is familiar. The truly remarkable thing about *Ulysses,* for instance, is the commonplaceness of its material. Of course there is much more in *Ulysses* than this, because Joyce is a kind of poet and also an elephantine pedant, but his real achievement has been to get the familiar on to paper. He dared—for it is a matter of *daring* just as much as of technique—to expose the imbecilities of the inner mind, and in doing so he discovered an America which was under everybody's nose. Here is a whole world of stuff which you supposed to be of its nature incommunicable, and somebody has managed to communicate it. The effect is to break down, at any rate momentarily, the solitude in which the human being lives. When you read certain passages in *Ulysses* you feel that Joyce's mind and your mind are one, that he knows all about you though he has never heard your name, that there exists some world outside time and space in which you and he are together. And though he does not resemble Joyce in other ways, there is a touch of this quality in Henry Miller. Not everywhere, because his work is very uneven, and sometimes, especially in *Black Spring,* tends to slide away into mere verbiage or into the squashy universe of the surrealists. But read him for five pages, ten pages, and you feel the peculiar relief that comes not so much from understanding as from *being understood.* "He knows all about me," you feel; "he wrote this specially for me." It is as though you could hear a voice speaking to you, a friendly American voice, with no humbug in it, no moral purpose, merely an implicit assumption that we are all alike. For the moment you have got away from the lies and simplifications, the stylised, marionette-like quality of ordinary fiction, even quite good fiction, and are dealing with the recognisable experiences of human beings.

But what kind of experience? What kind of human beings? Miller is writing about the man in the street, and it is incidentally rather a pity that it should be a street full of brothels. That is the penalty of leaving your native land. It means transferring your roots into shallower soil. Exile is probably more damaging to a novelist than to a painter or even a poet, because its effect is to take him out of contact with working life and narrow down his range to the street, the café, the church, the brothel and the studio. On the whole, in Miller's books you are reading about people living the expatriate life, people drinking, talking, meditating, and fornicating, not about people working, marrying, and bringing up children; a pity, because he would have described the one set of activities as well as the other. In *Black Spring* there is a wonderful flashback of New York, the swarming Irish-infested New York of the O. Henry period, but the Paris scenes are the best, and, granted their utter worthlessness as social types, the drunks and dead-beats of the cafés are handled with a feeling for character and a mastery of technique that are unapproached in any at all recent novel. All of them are not only credible but completely familiar; you have the feeling that all their adventures have happened to yourself. Not that they are anything very startling in the way of adventures. Henry gets a job with a melancholy Indian student, gets another job at a dreadful French school during a cold snap when the lavatories are frozen solid, goes on drinking bouts in Le Havre with his friend Collins, the sea captain, goes to brothels where there are wonderful Negresses, talks with his friend Van Norden, the novelist, who has got the great novel of the world in his head but can never bring himself to begin writing it. His friend Karl, on the verge of starvation, is picked up by a wealthy widow who wishes to marry him. There are interminable Hamlet-like conversations in which Karl tries to decide which is worse, being hungry or sleeping with an old woman. In great

detail he describes his visits to the widow, how he went to the
hotel dressed in his best, how before going in he neglected to
urinate, so that the whole evening was one long crescendo of torment, etc., etc. And after all, none of it is true, the widow doesn't
even exist—Karl has simply invented her in order to make himself seem important. The whole book is in this vein, more or less.
Why is it that these monstrous trivialities are so engrossing?
Simply because the whole atmosphere is deeply familiar, because
you have all the while the feeling that these things are happening
to *you*. And you have this feeling because somebody has chosen
to drop the Geneva language of the ordinary novel and drag the
real-politik of the inner mind into the open. In Miller's case it is
not so much a question of exploring the mechanisms of the mind
as of owning up to everyday facts and everyday emotions. For the
truth is that many ordinary people, perhaps an actual majority, do
speak and behave in just the way that is recorded here. The cal-
lous coarseness with which the characters in *Tropic of Cancer*
talk is very rare in fiction, but it is extremely common in real
life; again and again I have heard just such conversations from
people who were not even aware that they were talking coarsely.
It is worth noticing that *Tropic of Cancer* is not a young man's
book. Miller was in his forties when it was published, and though
since then he has produced three or four others, it is obvious that
this first book had been lived with for years. It is one of those
books that are slowly matured in poverty and obscurity, by people
who know what they have got to do and therefore are able to
wait. The prose is astonishing, and in parts of *Black Spring* is
even better. Unfortunately I cannot quote; unprintable words
occur almost everywhere. But get hold of *Tropic of Cancer,* get
hold of *Black Spring* and read especially the first hundred pages.
They give you an idea of what can still be done, even at this
late date, with English prose. In them, English is treated as a
spoken language, but spoken *without fear, i.e.* without fear of
rhetoric or of the unusual or poetical word. The adjective has
come back, after its ten years' exile. It is a flowing, swelling prose,
a prose with rhythms in it, something quite different from the
flat cautious statements and snackbar dialects that are now in
fashion.

When a book like *Tropic of Cancer* appears, it is only natural that the first thing people notice should be its obscenity. Given our current notions of literary decency, it is not at all easy to approach an unprintable book with detachment. Either one is shocked and disgusted, or one is morbidly thrilled, or one is determined above all else not to be impressed. The last is probably the commonest reaction, with the result that unprintable books often get less attention than they deserve. It is rather the fashion to say that nothing is easier than to write an obscene book, that people only do it in order to get themselves talked about and make money, etc., etc. What makes it obvious that this is *not* the case is that books which are obscene in the police-court sense are distinctly uncommon. If there were easy money to be made out of dirty words, a lot more people would be making it. But, because "obscene" books do not appear very frequently, there is a tendency to lump them together, as a rule quite unjustifiably. *Tropic of Cancer* has been vaguely associated with two other books, *Ulysses* and *Voyage au Bout de la Nuit,* but in neither case is there much resemblance. What Miller has in common with Joyce is a willingness to mention the inane squalid facts of everyday life. Putting aside differences of technique, the funeral scene in *Ulysses,* for instance, would fit into *Tropic of Cancer;* the whole chapter is a sort of confession, an *exposé* of the frightful inner callousness of the human being. But there the resemblance ends. As a novel, *Tropic of Cancer* is far inferior to *Ulysses.* Joyce is an artist, in a sense in which Miller is not and probably would not wish to be, and in any case he is attempting much more. He is exploring different states of consciousness, dream, reverie (the "bronze-by-gold" chapter), drunkenness, etc., and dovetailing them all into a huge complex pattern, almost like a Victorian "plot." Miller is simply a hard-boiled person talking about life, an ordinary American businessman with intellectual courage and a gift for words. It is perhaps significant that he *looks* exactly like everyone's idea of an American businessman. As for the comparison with *Voyage au Bout de la Nuit,* it is even further from the point. Both books use unprintable words, both are in some sense autobiographical, but that is all. *Voyage au Bout de la Nuit* is a book-with-a-purpose, and its purpose is to protest against the

horror and meaninglessness of modern life—actually, indeed, of
life. It is a cry of unbearable disgust, a voice from the cesspool.
Tropic of Cancer is almost exactly the opposite. The thing has
become so unusual as to seem almost anomalous, but it is the
book of a man who is happy. So is *Black Spring,* though slightly
less so, because tinged in places with nostalgia. With years of
lumpenproletarian life behind him, hunger, vagabondage, dirt,
failure, nights in the open, battles with immigration officers, endless struggles for a bit of cash, Miller finds that he is enjoying
himself. Exactly the aspects of life that fill Céline with horror
are the ones that appeal to him. So far from protesting, he is
accepting. And the very word "acceptance" calls up his real affinity, another American, Walt Whitman.

But there is something rather curious in being Whitman in
the nineteen-thirties. It is not certain that if Whitman himself
were alive at the moment he would write anything in the least
degree resembling *Leaves of Grass.* For what he is saying, after all,
is "I accept," and there is a radical difference between acceptance
now and acceptance then. Whitman was writing in a time of
unexampled prosperity, but more than that, he was writing in a
country where freedom was something more than a word. The
democracy, equality, and comradeship that he is always talking
about are not remote ideals, but something that existed in front
of his eyes. In midnineteenth-century America men felt themselves
free and equal, *were* free and equal, so far as that is possible outside a society of pure communism. There was poverty and there
were even class distinctions, but except for the Negroes there was
no permanently submerged class. Everyone had inside him, like a
kind of core, the knowledge that he could earn a decent living,
and earn it without bootlicking. When you read about Mark
Twain's Mississippi raftsmen and pilots, or Bret Harte's Western
gold-miners, they seem more remote than the cannibals of the
Stone Age. The reason is simply that they are free human beings.
But it is the same even with the peaceful domesticated America
of the Eastern states, the America of *Little Women, Helen's
Babies,* and *Riding Down from Bangor.* Life has a buoyant, care-
free quality that you can feel as you read, like a physical sensation
in your belly. It is this that Whitman is celebrating, though ac-

tually he does it very badly, because he is one of those writers who tell you what you ought to feel instead of making you feel it. Luckily for his beliefs, perhaps, he died too early to see the deterioration in American life that came with the rise of large-scale industry and the exploiting of cheap immigrant labour.

Miller's outlook is deeply akin to that of Whitman, and nearly everyone who has read him has remarked on this. *Tropic of Cancer* ends with an especially Whitmanesque passage, in which, after the lecheries, the swindles, the fights, the drinking bouts, and the imbecilities, he simply sits down and watches the Seine flowing past, in a sort of mystical acceptance of the thing-as-it-is. Only, what is he accepting? In the first place, not America, but the ancient boneheap of Europe, where every grain of soil has passed through innumerable human bodies. Secondly, not an epoch of expansion and liberty, but an epoch of fear, tyranny, and regimentation. To say "I accept" in an age like our own is to say that you accept concentration camps, rubber truncheons, Hitler, Stalin, bombs, aeroplanes, tinned food, machine guns, putsches, purges, slogans, Bedaux belts, gas masks, submarines, spies, provocateurs, press censorship, secret prisons, aspirins, Hollywood films, and political murders. Not *only* those things, of course, but those things among others. And on the whole this is Henry Miller's attitude. Not quite always, because at moments he shows signs of a fairly ordinary kind of literary nostalgia. There is a long passage in the earlier part of *Black Spring*, in praise of the Middle Ages, which as prose must be one of the most remarkable pieces of writing in recent years, but which displays an attitude not very different from that of Chesterton. In *Max and the White Phagocytes* there is an attack on modern American civilisation (breakfast cereals, cellophane, etc.) from the usual angle of the literary man who hates industrialism. But in general the attitude is "Let's swallow it whole." And hence the seeming preoccupation with indecency and with the dirtyhandkerchief side of life. It is only seeming, for the truth is that life consists far more largely of horrors than writers of fiction usually care to admit. Whitman himself "accepted" a great deal that his contemporaries found unmentionable. For he is not only writing of the prairie, he also wanders through the city and notes the shattered skull of the suicide, the "grey sick faces of onanists," etc., etc. But unquestionably our own age, at any rate in Western Europe, is less healthy and less hopeful than the age in which Whitman was writing. Unlike Whitman, we live in a *shrinking* world. The "democratic vistas" have ended in barbed wire. There is less feeling of creation and growth, less and less emphasis on the cradle, endlessly rocking, more and more emphasis on the teapot, endlessly stewing. To accept civilisation *as it is* practically means accepting decay. It has ceased to be a strenuous attitude and become a passive attitude—even "decadent," if that word means anything.

But precisely because, in one sense, he is passive to experience, Miller is able to get nearer to the ordinary man than is possible to more purposive writers. For the ordinary man is also passive. Within a narrow circle (home life, and perhaps the trade union or local politics) he feels himself master of his fate, but against major events he is as helpless as against the elements. So far from endeavouring to influence the future, he simply lies down and lets things happen to him. During the past ten years literature has involved itself more and more deeply in politics, with the result that there is now less room in it for the ordinary man than at any time during the past two centuries. One can see the change in the prevailing literary attitude by comparing the books written about the Spanish civil war with those written about the war of 1914-18. The immediately striking thing about the Spanish war books, at any rate those written in English, is their shocking dulness and badness. But what is more significant is that almost all of them, right-wing or left wing, are written from a political angle, by cocksure partisans telling you what to think, whereas the books about the Great War were written by common soldiers or junior officers who did not even pretend to understand what the whole thing was about. Books like *All Quiet on the Western Front, Le Feu, A Farewell to Arms, Death of a Hero, Good-bye to All that, Memoirs of an Infantry Officer,* and *A Subaltern on the Somme* were written not by propagandists but by *victims.* They are saying in effect, "What the hell is all this about? God knows. All we can do is to endure." And though he is not writing about war, nor, on the whole, about unhappiness, this is nearer to Miller's attitude than the omniscience which is now fashionable. The *Booster,* a shortlived periodical of which he was part-editor, used to describe itself in its advertisements as non-political, non-educational, non-progressive, non-cooperative, non-ethical, non-literary, non-consistent, non-contemporary," and Miller's own work could be described in nearly the same terms. It is a voice from the crowd, from the underling, from the third-class carriage, from the ordinary, non-political, non-moral, passive man.

I have been using the phrase "ordinary man" rather loosely, and I have taken it for granted that the "ordinary man" exists, a thing now denied by some people. I do not mean that the people Miller is writing about constitute a majority, still less that he is writing about proletarians. No English or American novelist has as yet seriously attempted that. And again, the people in *Tropic of Cancer* fall short of being ordinary to the extent that they are idle, disreputable, and more or less "artistic." As I have said already, this is a pity, but it is the necessary result of expatriation. Miller's "ordinary man" is neither the manual worker nor the suburban householder, but the derelict, the *déclassé,* the adventurer, the American intellectual without roots and without money. Still, the experiences even of this type overlap fairly widely with those of more normal people. Miller has been able to get the most out of his rather limited material because he has had the courage to identify with it. The ordinary man, the "average sensual man," has been given the power of speech, like Balaam's ass.

It will be seen that this is something out of date, or at any rate out of fashion. The average sensual man is out of fashion. Preoccupation with sex and truthfulness about the inner life are out of fashion. American Paris is out of fashion. A book like *Tropic of Cancer,* published at such a time, must be either a tedious preciosity or something unusual, and I think a majority of the people who have read it would agree that it is not the first. It is worth trying to discover just what this escape from the current literary fashion means. But to do that one has got to see it against its background—that is, against the general development of English literature in the twenty years since the Great War.

If this were a likely moment for the launching of "schools" of literature, Henry Miller might be the starting-point of a new "school." He does at any rate mark an unexpected swing of the pendulum. In his books one gets right away from the "political animal" and back to a viewpoint not only individualistic but completely passive—the viewpoint of a man who believes the world-process to be outside his control and who in any case hardly wishes to control it.

I first met Miller at the end of 1936, when I was passing through Paris on my way to Spain. What most intrigued me about him was to find that he felt no interest in the Spanish war whatever. He merely told me in forcible terms that to go to Spain at that moment was the act of an idiot. He could understand anyone going there from purely selfish motives, out of curiosity, for instance, but to mix oneself up in such things *from a sense of obligation* was sheer stupidity. In any case my ideas about combating Fascism, defending democracy, etc., etc., were all baloney. Our civilisation was destined to be swept away and replaced by something so different that we should scarcely regard it as human—a prospect that did not bother him, he said. And some such outlook is implicit throughout his work. Everywhere there is the sense of the approaching cataclysm, and almost everywhere the implied belief that it doesn't matter. The only political declaration which, so far as I know, he has ever made in print is a purely negative one. A year or so ago an American magazine, the *Marxist Quarterly,* sent out a questionnaire to various American writers asking them to define their attitude on the subject of war. Miller replied in terms of extreme pacifism, an individual refusal to fight, with no apparent wish to convert others to the same opinion—practically, in fact, a declaration of irresponsibility.

However, there is more than one kind of irresponsibility. As a rule, writers who do not wish to identify themselves with the historical process of the moment either ignore it or fight against it. If they can ignore it, they are probably fools. If they can understand it well enough to want to fight against it, they probably have enough vision to realise that they cannot win. Look, for instance, at a poem like "The Scholar Gypsy," with its railing against the "strange disease of modern life" and its magnificent defeatist simile in the final stanza. It expresses one of the normal literary attitudes, perhaps actually the prevailing attitude during the last hundred years. And on the other hand there are the "progressives," the yeasayers, the Shaw-Wells type, always leaping forward to embrace the ego-projections which they mistake for the future. On the whole the writers of the 'twenties took the first line and the writers of the 'thirties the second. And at any given moment, of course, there is a huge tribe of Barries and Deepings and Dells who simply don't notice what is happening. Where Miller's work is symptomatically important is in its avoidance of any of these attitudes. He is neither pushing the world-process forward nor trying to drag it back, but on the other hand he is by no means ignoring it. I should say that he believes in the impending ruin of Western Civilisation much more firmly than the majority of "revolutionary" writers; only he does not feel called upon to do anything about it. He is fiddling while Rome is burning, and, unlike the enormous majority of people who do this, fiddling with his face towards the flames.

In *Max and the White Phagocytes* there is one of those revealing passages in which a writer tells you a great deal about himself while talking about somebody else. The book includes a long essay on the diaries of Anaïs Nin, which I have never read, except for a few fragments, and which I believe have not been published. Miller claims that they are the only true feminine writing that has ever appeared, whatever that may mean. But the interesting passage is one in which he compares Anaïs Nin—evidently a completely subjective, introverted writer—to Jonah in the whale's belly. In passing he refers to an essay that Aldous Huxley wrote some years ago about El Greco's picture, *The Dream of Philip the Second*. Huxley remarks that the people in El Greco's pictures always look as though they were in the bellies of whales, and professes to find something peculiarly horrible in the idea of being in a "visceral prison." Miller retorts that, on the contrary, there are many worse things than being swallowed by whales, and the passage makes it clear that he himself finds the idea rather attractive. Here he is touching upon what is probably a very widespread fantasy. It is perhaps worth noticing that everyone, at least every English-speaking person, invariably speaks of Jonah and the *whale*. Of course the creature that swallowed Jonah was a fish, and is so described in the Bible (Jonah, 1:17), but children naturally confuse it with a whale, and this fragment of baby-talk is habitually carried into later life—a sign, perhaps, of the hold that the Jonah myth has upon our imaginations. For the fact is that being inside a whale is a very comfortable, cosy, home-like thought. The historical Jonah, if he can be so called, was glad enough to escape, but in imagination, in day-dream, count-less people have envied him. It is, of course, quite obvious why. The whale's belly is simply a womb big enough for an adult. There you are, in the dark, cushioned space that exactly fits you, with yards of blubber between yourself and reality, able to keep up an attitude of the completest indifference, no matter *what* happens. A storm that would sink all the battleships in the world would hardly reach you as an echo. Even the whale's own move-ments would probably be imperceptible to you. He might be wal-lowing among the surface waves or shooting down into the black-ness of the middle seas (a mile deep, according to Herman Melville), but you would never notice the difference. Short of being dead, it is the final, unsurpassable stage of irresponsibility. And however it may be with Anaïs Nin, there is no question that Miller himself is inside the whale. All his best and most characteristic passages are written from the angle of Jonah, a willing Jonah. Not that he is especially introverted—quite the contrary. In his case the whale happens to be transparent. Only he feels no impulse to alter or control the process that he is under-going. He has performed the essential Jonah act of allowing him-self to be swallowed, remaining passive, *accepting*.

It will be seen what this amounts to. It is a species of quiet-ism, implying either complete unbelief or else a degree of belief amounting to mysticism. The attitude is "Je m'en fous" or "Though He slay me, yet will I trust in Him," whichever way you like to look at it; for practical purposes both are identical, the moral in either case being "Sit on your bum." But in a time like ours, is this a defensible attitude? Notice that it is almost impossible to refrain from asking this question. At the moment of writing we are still in a period in which it is taken for granted that books ought always to be positive, serious, and "constructive." A dozen years ago this idea would have been greeted with titters ("My dear aunt, one doesn't write *about* anything, one just *writes."*) Then the pendulum swung away from the frivolous notion that art is merely technique, but it swung a very long distance, to the point of asserting that a book can only be "good" if it is founded on a "true" vision of life. Naturally the people who believe this also believe that they are in possession of the truth themselves. Catholic critics, for instance, tend to claim that books are only "good" when they are of Catholic tendency. Marxist critics make the same claim more boldly for Marxist books. For instance, Mr. Edward Upward ("A Marxist Interpretation of Literature," in *The Mind in Chains*):

> Literary criticism which aims at being Marxist must . . . proclaim that no book written *at the present time* can be "good" unless it is written from a Marxist or near-Marxist viewpoint.

Various other writers have made similar or comparable statements. Mr. Upward italicises "at the present time" because he realises that you cannot, for instance, dismiss *Hamlet* on the ground that Shakespeare was not a Marxist. Nevertheless his interesting essay only glances very shortly at this difficulty. Much of the literature that comes to us out of the past is permeated by and in fact founded on beliefs (the belief in the immortality of the soul, for example) which now seem to us false and in some cases contemptably silly. Yet it is "good" literature, if survival is any test. Mr. Upward would no doubt answer that a belief which was appropriate several centuries ago might be inappropriate and therefore stultifying now. But this does not get one much farther, because it assumes that in any age there will be *one* body of belief which is the current approximation to truth, and that the best literature of the time will be more or less in harmony with it. Actually no such uniformity has ever existed. In seventeenth-century England, for instance, there was a religious and political cleavage which distinctly resembled the left-right antagonism of today. Looking back, most modern people would feel that the bourgeois-Puritan viewpoint was a better approximation to truth than the Catholic-feudal one. But it is certainly not the case that all or even a majority of the best writers of the time were Puritans. And more than this, there exist "good" writers whose world-view would in *any* age be recognised as false and silly. Edgar Allan Poe is an example. Poe's outlook is at best a wild romanticism and at worst is not far from being insane in the literal clinical sense. Why is it, then, that stories like *The Black Cat, The Tell-tale Heart, The Fall of the House of Usher* and so forth, which might very nearly have been written by a lunatic, do not convey a feeling of falsity? Because they are true within a certain framework, they keep the rules of their own peculiar world, like a Japanese picture. But it appears that to write successfully about such a world you have got to believe in it. One sees the difference immediately if one compares Poe's *Tales* with what is, in my opinion, an insincere attempt to work up a similar atmosphere, Julian Green's *Minuit*. The thing that immediately strikes one about *Minuit* is that there is no reason why any of the events in it should happen. Everything is completely arbitrary; there is no emotional sequence. But this is exactly what one does *not* feel with Poe's stories. Their maniacal logic, in its own setting, is quite convincing. When, for instance, the drunkard seizes the black cat and cuts its eye out with his penknife, one knows exactly *why* he did it, even to the point of feeling that one would have done the same oneself. It seems therefore that for a creative writer possession of the "truth" is less important than emotional sincerity. Even Mr. Upward would not claim that a writer needs nothing beyond a Marxist training. He also needs talent. But talent, apparently, is a matter of being able to *care,* of really *believing* in your beliefs, whether they are true or false. The difference between, for instance, Céline and Evelyn Waugh is a difference of emotional intensity. It is the difference between genuine despair and a despair that is at least partly a pretence. And with this there goes another consideration which is perhaps less obvious: that there are occasions when an "untrue" belief is more likely to be sincerely held than a "true" one.

If one looks at the books of personal reminiscence written about the war of 1914-18, one notices that nearly all that have remained readable after a lapse of time are written from a passive, negative angle. They are the records of something completely meaningless, a nightmare happening in a void. That was not actually the truth about the war, but it was the truth about the individual reaction. The soldier advancing into a machine-gun barrage or standing waist-deep in a flooded trench knew only that here was an appalling experience in which he was all but helpless. He was likelier to make a good book out of his helplessness and his ignorance than out of a pretended power to see the whole thing in perspective. As for the books that were written during the war itself, the best of them were nearly all the work of people who simply turned their backs and tried not to notice that the war was happening. Mr. E. M. Forster has described how in 1917 he read *Prufrock* and others of Eliot's early poems, and how it heartened him at such a time to get hold of poems that were "innocent of public-spiritedness":

> They sang of private disgust and diffidence, and of people who seemed genuine because they were unattractive or weak. . . . Here was a protest, and a feeble one, and the more congenial for being feeble. . . . He who could turn aside to complain of ladies and drawing rooms preserved a tiny drop of our self-respect, he carried on the human heritage.

That is very well said. Mr. MacNeice, in the book I have referred to already, quotes this passage and somewhat smugly adds:

> Ten years later less feeble protests were to be made by poets and the human heritage carried on rather differently. . . . The contemplation of a world of fragments becomes boring and Eliot's successors are more interested in tidying it up.

Similar remarks are scattered throughout Mr. MacNeice's book. What he wishes us to believe is that Eliot's "successors" (meaning Mr. MacNeice and his friends) have in some way "protested" more effectively than Eliot did by publishing *Prufrock* at the moment when the Allied armies were assaulting the Hindenburg Line. Just where these "protests" are to be found I do not know. But in the contrast between Mr. Forster's comment and Mr. MacNeice's lies all the difference between a man who knows what the 1914-18 war was like and a man who barely remembers it. The truth is that in 1917 there was nothing that a thinking and a sensitive person could do, except to remain human, if possible. And a gesture of helplessness, even of frivolity, might be the best way of doing that. If I had been a soldier fighting in the Great War, I would sooner have got hold of *Prufrock* than *The First Hundred Thousand* or Horatio Bottomley's *Letters to the Boys in the Trenches*. I should have felt, like Mr. Forster, that by simply standing aloof and keeping touch with pre-war emotions, Eliot was carrying on the human heritage. What a relief it would have been at such a time, to read about the hesitations of a middle-aged highbrow with a bald spot! So different from bayonet-drill! After the bombs and the food-queues and the recruiting-posters, a human voice! What a relief!

But, after all, the war of 1914-18 was only a heightened moment in an almost continuous crisis. At this date it hardly even needs a war to bring home to us the disintegration of our society and the increasing helplessness of all decent people. It is for this reason that I think that the passive, non-cooperative attitude implied in Henry Miller's work is justified. Whether or not it is an expression of what people *ought* to feel, it probably comes somewhere near to expressing what they *do* feel. Once again it is the human voice among the bomb-explosions, a friendly American voice, "innocent of public-spiritedness." No sermons, merely the subjective truth. And along these lines, apparently, it is still possible for a good novel to be written. Not necessarily an edifying novel, but a novel worth reading and likely to be remembered after it is read.

While I have been writing this essay another European war has broken out. It will either last several years and tear Western

civilisation to pieces, or it will end inconclusively and prepare
the way for yet another war which will do the job once and for
all. But war is only "peace intensified." What is quite obviously
happening, war or no war, is the break-up of laissez-faire capitalism and of the liberal-Christian culture. Until recently the full
implications of this were not foreseen, because it was generally
imagined that socialism could preserve and even enlarge the
atmosphere of liberalism. It is now beginning to be realised how
false this idea was. Almost certainly we are moving into an age
of totalitarian dictatorships—an age in which freedom of thought
will be at first a deadly sin and later on a meaningless abstraction.
The autonomous individual is going to be stamped out of existence. But this means that literature, in the form in which we know
it, must suffer at least a temporary death. The literature of liberalism is coming to an end and the literature of totalitarianism has
not yet appeared and is barely imaginable. As for the writer, he
is sitting on a melting iceberg; he is merely an anachronism, a
hangover from the bourgeois age, as surely doomed as the hippo-
potamus. Miller seems to me a man out of the common because
he saw and proclaimed this fact a long while before most of his
contemporaries—at a time, indeed, when many of them were
actually burbling about a renaissance of literature. Wyndham
Lewis had said years earlier that the major history of the English
language was finished, but he was basing this on different and
rather trivial reasons. But from now onwards the all-important
fact for the creative writer is going to be that this is not a writer's
world. That does not mean that he cannot help to bring the
new society into being, but he can take no part in the process *as a
writer*. For *as a writer* he is a liberal, and what is happening is
the destruction of liberalism. It seems likely, therefore, that in
the remaining years of free speech any novel worth reading will
follow more or less along the lines that Miller has followed—I
do not mean in technique or subject matter, but in implied outlook. The passive attitude will come back, and it will be more
consciously passive than before. Progress and reaction have both
turned out to be swindles. Seemingly there is nothing left but
quietism—robbing reality of its terrors by simply submitting to
it. Get inside the whale—or rather, admit you are inside the

whale (for you *are,* of course). Give yourself over to the world-process, stop fighting against it or pretending that you control it; simply accept it, endure it, record it. That seems to be the formula that any sensitive novelist is now likely to adopt. A novel on more positive, "constructive" lines, and not emotionally spurious, is at present very difficult to imagine.

But do I mean by this that Miller is a "great author," a new hope for English prose? Nothing of the kind. Miller himself would be the last to claim or want any such thing. No doubt he will go on writing—anybody who has once started always goes on writing—and associated with him there are a number of writers of approximately the same tendency, Lawrence Durrell, Michael Fraenkel and others, almost amounting to a "school." But he himself seems to me essentially a man of one book. Sooner or later I should expect him to descend into unintelligibility, or into charlatanism; there are signs of both in his later work. His last book, *Tropic of Capricorn,* I have not even read. This was not because I did not want to read it, but because the police and customs authorities have so far managed to prevent me from getting hold of it. But it would surprise me if it came anywhere near *Tropic of Cancer* or the opening chapters of *Black Spring.* Like certain other autobiographical novelists, he had it in him to do just one thing perfectly, and he did it. Considering what the fiction of the nineteen-thirties has been like, that is something.

Miller's books are published by the Obelisk Press in Paris. What will happen to the Obelisk Press, now that war has broken out and Jack Kahane, the publisher, is dead, I do not know, but at any rate the books are still procurable. I earnestly counsel anyone who has not done so to read at least *Tropic of Cancer.* With a little ingenuity, or by paying a little over the published price, you can get hold of it, and even if parts of it disgust you, it will stick in your memory. It is also an "important" book, in a sense different from the sense in which that word is generally used. As a rule novels are spoken of as "important" when they are either a "terrible indictment" of something or other or when they introduce some technical innovation. Neither of these applies to *Tropic of Cancer.* Its importance is merely symptomatic. Here in my opinion is the only imaginative prose-writer of the slightest value who has appeared among the English-speaking races for some years past. Even if that is objected to as an overstatement, it will probably be admitted that Miller is a writer out of the ordinary, worth more than a single glance; and after all, he is a completely negative, unconstructive, amoral writer, a mere Jonah, a passive acceptor of evil, a sort of Whitman among the corpses. Symptomatically, that is more significant than the mere fact that five thousand novels are published in England every year and four thousand nine hundred of them are tripe. It is a demonstration of the *impossibility* of any major literature until the world has shaken itself into its new shape.

HENRY MILLER: *IMAGE AND IDEA*

Philip Rahv

If Henry Miller's status in our literary community is still so very debatable, it is probably because he is the type of writer who cannot help exposing himself to extreme appraisals with every page that he adds to his collected works. Hs is easily overrated and with equal ease run down or ignored altogether. Consider his present situation. With few exceptions the highbrow critics, bred almost to a man in Eliot's school of strict impersonal aesthetics, are bent on snubbing him. What with his spellbinder's tone, bawdy rites, plebeian rudeness and disdain of formal standards, he makes bad copy for them and they know it. His admirers, on the other hand, are so hot-lipped in praise as to arouse the suspicion of a cultist attachment. They evade the necessity of drawing distinctions between the art of exploiting one's personality and the art of exploiting material, from whatever source, for creative purposes. And in Miller's case such distinctions are very much in order. His work is so flagrantly personal in content that in moments of acute irritation one is tempted to dismiss it as so much personality-mongering. Repeatedly he has declared that his concern is not with writing as generally understood but with telling the "more and more inexhaustible" story of his life—a story stretched to include a full recital of his opinions, philo-

sophic rhapsodies, intuitions, hunches, and buffooneries. All too
often he plunges into that maudlin boosting of the ego to which
the bohemian character is generally disposed. Yet at his best he
writes on a level of true expressiveness, generating a kind of all-
out poetry, at once genial and savage.

Unfortunately, since finishing off his expatriation and returning to his native country he has given more and more free
rein to his worst tendency, that of playing the philosopher on a
binge and the gadabout of the California avant-garde. The last
book of his in which his great talent is shown to best advantage is
The Colossus of Maroussi, published in 1942. It is a travel book
on Greece of a very special type. Though containing some plain
information about the country and its inhabitants, it intrinsically
belongs to the modern tradition of the fugitives from progress—
from the lands ravaged by the machine, the salesman, and the
abstract thinker—the tradition of Melville and Gauguin in Ta-
hiti and D. H. Lawrence in Mexico and Taos. Miller went to
Greece to purge himself of his long contact with the French and
to make good his hope for spiritual renewal. "In Greece," he
writes, "I finally achieved coordination. I became deflated, re-
stored to proper human proportions, ready to accept my lot and
to give of all that I have received. Standing in Agamemnon's
tomb I went through a veritable rebirth." He speaks of the Greeks
as "aimless, anarchic, thoroughly and discordantly human," thus
identifying them closely with his own values; and though con-
fessing that he never read a line of Homer, he none the less believes them to be essentially unchanged.

Where he shows an unusual aptitude for descriptive prose
is in the account of his visits to Mycenae, Knossus, Phaestos, and
other sites of antiquity. Some of the passages are very good examples of his rhetorical prowess. Hyperbolic statement is his natural
mode of communication, yet he has a vital sense of reference to
concrete objects and symbols which permits him to gain a measure
of control over his swelling language. He is particularly addicted
to using terms and images drawn from science, especially biology
and astronomy; and his unvarying practice is to distribute these
borrowings stylistically in a manner so insinuating as to produce
effects of incongruity and alarm. It is a device perfectly expressive

of his fear of science and all its works. For Miller belongs to the progress-hating and machine-smashing fraternity of contemporary letters, though lacking as he does the motive of allegiance to tradition, it is open to question whether his co-thinkers would ever assent to his company. Of late, too, he has increasingly yielded to his mystical leanings, and his mysticism is of the wholesale kind, without limit or scruple. Thus there is a curious chapter in *The Colossus of Maroussi* describing his interview with an Armenian soothsayer in Athens, who confirms Miller in his belief that he is never going to die and that he is destined to undertake missions of a messianic nature that will "bring great joy to the world." Now this is the sort of thing that can be taken, of course, either as a fancy piece of megalomania or as a legitimate aspiration to which every human being is entitled.

But if Miller's recent work has been disappointing, the one way to recover a sense of his significance is to go back to his three early novels—*Tropic of Cancer, Black Spring,* and *Tropic of Capricorn.* These novels are autobiographical, and he appears in them in the familiar role of the artist-hero who dominates modern fiction. Where he differs from this ubiquitous type is in the extremity of his destitution and estrangement from society. Reduced to the status of a lumpen-proletarian whom the desolation of the big city has finally drained of all illusions and ideals, he is now an utterly declassed and alienated man who lives his life in the open streets of Paris and New York.

In these novels the narrator's every contact with cultural objects serves merely to exacerbate his anarchic impulses. There no longer exists for him any shelter from the external world. Even the idea of home—a place that the individual can truly call his own because it is furnished not only with his belongings but with his very humanity—has been obliterated. What remains is the fantasy of returning to the womb, a fantasy so obsessive as to give rise to an elaborate intra-uterine imagery as well as to any number of puns, jokes, imprecations, and appeals.

It is precisely in his descriptions of his lumpen-proletarian life in the streets that Miller is at his best, that his prose is most resonant and alive—the streets in which a never ending array of decomposed and erratic phenomena gives his wanderings in search of a woman or a meal the metaphysical sheen of dream and legend. In every shopwindow he sees the "sea-nymph squirming in the maniac's arms," and everywhere he smells the odor of love "gushing like sewergas" out of the leading mains: "Love without gender and without lysol, incubational love, such as the wolverines practice above the treeline." In these novels food and sex are thematically treated with such matter-of-fact exactitude, with such a forceful and vindictive awareness of rock-bottom needs, that they cease to mean what they mean to most of us. Miller invokes food and sex as heroic sentiments and even generalizes them into principles. For the man who is down and out has eyes only for that which he misses most frequently; his condition makes of him a natural anarchist, rendering irrelevant all conventions, moral codes, or any attempt to order the process of experience according to some value-pattern. The problem is simply to keep alive, and to that end all means are permissible. One turns into a desperado, lurking in ambush in hallways, bars, and hotel rooms in the hope that some stroke of luck will enable one "to make a woman or make a touch." He literally takes candy from babies and steals money from prostitutes. As for obtaining regular work, he was always able "to amuse, to nourish, to instruct, but never to be accepted in a genuine way . . . everything conspired to set me off as an *outlaw*."

The fact that the world is in a state of collapse fills him with deep gratification ("I am dazzled by the glorious collapse of the world") because the all-around ruin seems to justify and validate what has happened to him personally. His particular adjustment he accomplishes by accepting the collapse as a kind of apocalyptic show from which the artist who has been rejected by society, and whose role is to revive the primeval, chaotic instincts, might even expect to gain the resurgence of those dreams and myths that the philistines have done their utmost to suppress. It is senseless to interfere, to try to avert the catastrophe; all one can do is to recoil into one's private fate. "The world is what it is and I am what I am," he declares. "I expose myself to the destructive elements that surround me. I let everything wreak its own havoc with me. I bend over to spy on the secret processes to obey rather than to command." And again: "I'm neither for nor against, I'm neutral. . . . If to live is the paramount thing, then I will live even if I become a cannibal." And even in his own proper sphere the artist is no longer free to construct objective forms. He must abandon the "literary gold standard" and devote himself to creating biographical works—human documents rather than "literature"—depicting man in the grip of delirium.

And Miller's practice fits his theory. His novels do in fact dissolve the forms and genres of writing in a stream of exhortation, narrative, world-historical criticism, prose-poetry and spontaneous philosophy, all equally subjected to the strain and grind of self-expression at all costs. So riled is his ego by external reality, so confused and helpless, that he can no longer afford the continual sacrifice of personality that the act of creation requires, he can no longer bear to express himself implicitly by means of the work of art as a whole but must simultaneously permeate and absorb each of its separate parts and details. If everything else has failed me, this author seems to say, at least this book is mine, here everything is fashioned in my own image, here I am God.

This is the meaning, I think, of the "biographical" aesthetic that Miller at once practiced and preached in his early work and which an increasing number of writers, though not cognizant of it as a program, nevertheless practice in the same compulsive manner, not necessarily for reasons as personal as Miller's or with the same results, but because the growing alienation of man in modern society throws them back into narcissistic attitudes, forces them to undertake the shattering task of possessing the world that is now full of abstractions and mystifications through the instrumentality of the self and the self alone. Not "Know Thyself!" but "Be Yourself!" is their motto. Thomas Wolfe was such a writer, and his career was frustrated by the fact that he lacked sufficient consciousness to understand his dilemma. Miller, on the other hand, was well aware of his position when writing his early fictions. Instead of attempting to recover the lost relation to the world, he accepted his alienated status as his inexorable fate, and by so doing he was able to come to some kind of terms with it.

If freedom is the recognition of necessity, then what Miller gained was the freedom to go the whole length in the subversion of values, to expose more fully perhaps than any other contemporary novelist in English the nihilism of the self which has been cut off from all social ties and released not only from an allegiance to the past but also from all commitments to the future. The peculiarly American affirmation voiced by Whitman was thus completely negated in Miller. Total negation instead of total affirmation! No wonder that like Wolfe and Hart Crane and other lost souls he was continually haunted by Whitman as by an apparition. In *Tropic of Cancer* he speaks of him as "the one lone figure which America has produced in the course of her brief life . . . the first and last poet . . . who is almost undecipherable today, a monument covered with rude hieroglyphs for which there is no key." And it is precisely because he had the temerity to go the whole length that Miller is important as a literary character, though his importance, as George Orwell has observed, may be more symptomatic than substantial, in the sense that the extreme of passivity, amoralism, and acceptance of evil that his novels represent tends to demonstrate "the impossibility of any major literature until the world has shaken itself into a new shape."

In all his books Miller apostrophizes the Dadists, the Surrealists and the seekers and prophets of the "marvelous," wherever they may be found. Perhaps because he discovered the avant-gardists so late in life, he is naive enough to take their system of verbal ferocity at its face value and to adopt their self-inflationary mannerisms and outcries. At the same time he likes to associate himself with D. H. Lawrence, who was not at all an avant-gardist in the Parisian group sense of the term. He apparently regards himself as Lawrence's successor. But the truth is that they have very little in common, and there is no better way of showing it than by comparing their approaches to the sexual theme.

Miller is above all morally passive in his novels, whereas Lawrence, though he too was overwhelmed by the alienation of modern man, was sustained throughout by his supreme gift for moral activity; and he was sufficiently high-visioned to believe that a change of heart was possible, that he could reverse the current that had so long been running in one direction. Hence his idea of sexual fulfillment as a means of reintegration. Miller, however, in whose narratives sex forms the main subject-matter, presents sexual relations almost without exception in terms of fornication, which are precisely the terms that Lawrence simply loathed. The innumerable seductions, so casual and joyless, that Miller describes with such insistence on reproducing all the ribald and obscene details, are almost entirely on the level of street encounters. He has none of Molly Bloom's earthiness, nor does he ever quake with Lawrence's holy tremors. He treats erotic functions with a kind of scabrous humor, for there is scarcely any feeling in him for the sex-partner as a human being. What he wants is once and for all to expose "the conjugal orgy in the Black Hole of Calcutta." Not that he is open to the charge of pornography; on the contrary, behind his concentration on sexual experience there is a definite literary motive, or rather a double motive: first, the use of this experience to convey a sense of cultural and social disorder, to communicate a nihilist outlook, and second, an insatiable naturalistic curiosity. It is plain that Miller and Lawrence are opposites rather than twins.

Miller's claims as a guide to life and letters or as a prophet of doom can be easily discounted, though one remembers an essay by him on Proust and Joyce, called "The Universe of Death," which is a truly inspired piece of criticism. In his three novels, however, he is remarkable as the biographer of the hobo-intellectual and as the poet of those people at the bottom of society in whom some unforeseen or surreptitious contact with art and literature has aroused a latent antagonism to ordinary living, a resolve to escape the treadmill even at the cost of hunger and degradation. In dealing with this material, Miller has performed a new act of selection. There is in his fiction, also, a Dickensian strain of caricature which comes to the surface again and again, as in the riotously funny monologues of the journalists Carl and Van Norden in *Tropic of Cancer*. The truth is that his bark is worse than his bite. He strikes the attitudes of a wild man, but what he lacks is the murderous logic and purity of his European prototypes. Though he can be as ferocious as Céline, he is never so consistent; and the final impression we have of his novels is that of a naturally genial and garrulous American who has been through hell. But now that he has had a measure of recognition and has settled down at home to receive the homage of his admirers he seems to have entered a new phase, and his work only occasionally reminds us of the role of bohemian desperado which in his expatriate years he assumed with complete authority and conviction.

SHADOW OF DOOM: AN ESSAY ON HENRY MILLER

Wallace Fowlie

I believe that the quality which first attracted me in Mr. Miller's writing was his violence. Not the violence of things said, but the violence of the way in which they were said. The violence of feeling has become in his work the violence of style which has welded together all of his disparate passions and dispersed experiences into the one experience of language. He has said in *The Wisdom of the Heart* that he doesn't believe in words, but in language, "which is something beyond words" (p. 23). Writing is a kind of complete celebration for him in which shattered parts of experience are put together, in which elements are fused. Thees elements are not, however, fused into a system of thought and experience which can be learned or understood. They can only be "realized," more and more intuitively. Miller reveals in his art, to a remarkable degree, the gift of immediacy. His hungers of the present are never over. They never become past hungers to be recalled. From this vision of life, which is one self-perpetuating uninterrupted experience, comes his writing, integrated with the flowing steadiness of life, pulsating with the newness and the sameness of each day, incapable of being codified and explicated in accordance with the rules of "periods," of "genres," of "themes."

35

In rereading recently the brilliant correspondence exchanged between Henry Miller and Michael Fraenkel, published under the title *Hamlet,* I had, more clearly than ever, the conviction that Miller is a leading example of a special kind of writer produced only by our age. I mean the writer who is essentially seer and prophet, whose immediate ancestor was Rimbaud and whose leading exponent was D. H. Lawrence. It is not insignificant that Henry Miller considers the poet whose perceptions and visions blotted out his language, Arthur Rimbaud, one of the greatest writers, and that he is now engaged upon the writing of a critical study of Lawrence.

What characterizes this new artist is perhaps his vulnerability to experiences. He exposes himself to them all in a kind of pro-pitiatory frenzy as though he needs literally to know everything before he can understand adequately any single part of human experience. In a more histrionic sense than ever before, the mod-ern artist is the scapegoat who feels physically the weight of the world's sins and who performs in his life the role of the clown. He relives all the incarnations of the hero which he calls, in his more modest language, his masks. His roles are as multiple as his genres. Rimbaud called himself: "saltimbanque, mendiant, artiste, bandit,—petre!" (juggler, beggar, artist, bandit,—priest: Une Saison en Enfer). Lawrence wrote novels, short stories, essays, poems, plays, books of travel and philosophy. Henry Miller's writing is autobiography, fiction, philosophy, criticism. He is, in a special sense which we shall try to define, novelist, saint, critic, voluptuary, and perhaps now destined to be a poet.

The word schizophrenia is hardly sufficient to define the divis-ionings of the modern artist's sensitivity and the seemingly auton-omous realms of his action. The Hamlet complex appears rudi-mentary when viewed from the intricately partitioned experience of a Rimbaud, of a Lawrence, and of a Henry Miller! The reasons for this reduplicated role of the artist are difficult to state because they are so deeply imbedded in the spiritual problems of our age which, although they explain us, do not explain themselves to us. But perhaps we see enough to realize that our age of defeat over which man, if he is to exist at all as an artist, must triumph. This triumph of the modern artist over his defeated age was once called an escape or, by the more clinical word, escapism. We know better now. The age whose parts are so ill-fused and dislocated has had to be dominated, not by the solitary man in his ivory tower, a term of castigation exploited by politicians and all the lesser breeds of men, but by the artist who has had to reassemble in himself all the shattered parts of the world.

The modern artist, more admirably and more insistently than ever before in the history of art, is the fusion of dreamer and hero. Because of the wounded and divided age in which he lives, he has become the fusion of the enemy brothers Dionysus and Apollo. The ardor of Dionysus and the wisdom of Apollo,—that is, the body and the spirit, the earth and the sun, woman and man,— have been united in the modern artist in remarkably even proportions. In the creation of his art, the artist always begins with Dionysus and moves toward Apollo. That is, he always begins with chaos and moves toward order. It is impossible to have in art solely the orgiasm of Dionysus or solely the elevation of Apollo. The faun who plays on the flute is an excellent example of what I mean. The image of the orgiastic faun learning to know order and harmony describes the legend of all creative art.

Our divided and impaired age has produced in spite of itself such unified and triumphant artists as Proust, Joyce, Lawrence, and Henry Miller, who have transcended it by being of it more creatively and more spiritually than the age's so-called and falsely-denominated "leaders." These writers, in each of their books, have done two things. They have written their own autobiography and they have composed the history of their age. They have been accused of retreating to their ivory tower and turning their backs on the politics of the moment, but in reality, they were approaching more and more closely to the meaning of their age. They were learning less and realizing more. Rather than trying to rule the world with greed and emasculated philosophies, they were learning how to accept the world. The acceptance of the world is the first necessary triumph which precedes the love of the world and the love of the world's Creator.

In his frank acceptance of the world, the modern artist learned to perceive in it the forces of evil as well as the forces of good, and hence to prepare himself for the particular role of

prophet which he has played so consistently and so brilliantly. The
very title of Mr. Miller's book, *The Wisdom of the Heart,* is a
key to the artist's function, and in it, on page 45, there is a
sentence which might well be a sermon text for this essay: "We
are in the grip of demonic forces created by our own fear and
ignorance." The little man who is terrified and who is in reality
greater than that which terrifies him is the choreographic objecti-
fication of the artist. He is the homunculus who is physically
crushed by the world but who spiritually dominates the world
in his quest for the absolute. The heroes who Henry Miller talks
about the most are all the same type of passionate clown: Rimbaud and Lawrence, Charlie Chaplin and Raimu, Gary Cooper as
Mr. Deeds, Christ and Saint Francis, Miller himself as the hero
in *The Tropic of Cancer.* When he writes about the French, it is
always about the little man and the insignificant—who is, nevertheless, the microscopic greatness of a civilization: the garçon de
cafe, the store proprietor, the whore, the pimp (cf. Vive la France
in Hemispheres, Nos. 2-3, 1944).

On the homunculus falls more tragically than on the proud
and successful the shadow of doom announced by Spengler and
Lawrence. To a certain extent, Henry Miller continues the prophetic role of these two writers, but preaches infinitely less. Oswald
Spengler, the prophet of cyclical history, D. H. Lawrence, the
psychologist of love and sex, and Henry Miller, the visionary
who perceives his wisdom in the microcosm of the heart, are all
contained in the boy-prophet Arthur Rimbaud. The French poet
discovered a meaning in the cycles of history and races before
Spengler, and attained the virile purity which Lawrence sought
to reestablish in the body of man, and played under his masks of
hyena, convict, and pagan the role of Miller's homunculus who
sees because he suffers.

So the shadow of doom announced by the modern prophets
and which is falling over all of humanity today, was first articu-
lated in the voice of Rimbaud which continues to speak in the
visionaries who have succeeded him, of whom Henry Miller is
perhaps the leading contemporary. The prophet and the visionary
is the man who daily lives the metaphysical problems of his age.
He bears them in him and undergoes their suffering. Writing be-

comes for him, then, a very special and necessary torture. A daily expiation for his age which he performs innocently and ineluctably. The metaphysical torment of today which Miller seems to feel the most persistently is the loss throughout the world of the great fact of living. In the manifold ways and patterns of living which modern man is always inventing, he has forgotten that to live is of the prime importance.

How to live is the theme of all prophets. Peace is always the goal; and around the word "peace" cluster the plans and the dreams, the intuitions and the burning designs of those men who see into the heart of the living and into the future. The peace of the world is for Henry Miller associated with Paris because there it is more possible for man, so divided in his natural heritage of today, to become one as artist. In their creative activity, even if not always in their lives as men, some of the most notable among contemporary artists have attained a unity thanks to the spiritual role of Paris, last of the great modern cities where it was possible to live without spending one's life devising ways and policies of living. It is impossible to measure the peace of Paris in the works of Frenchmen like Proust, Cocteau, Rouault; of the Irish James Joyce; of the Russian Chagall and Tchelitchew; of the Spanish Picasso; of the American Gertrude Stein, Hemingway, and Henry Miller. From some wellspring of ancient liberty, Paris has safeguarded a fertile power in the unity of her native and assimilated artists who, not only in the accomplishment of their work but in their understanding of man, defy the usual contemporary waywardness and bifurcations.

As an artist, Miller has been able to see the discordant elements of our world to such a degree of clarity that he has freed himself from them. He has attained in his writing to the purity of obscenity, as Proust attained to the purity of immorality, as Baudelaire attained to the purity of acedia, as Dante attained to the purity of hell. There has been throughout the history of American literature an uninterrupted preoccupation with the theme of evil, treated from a special viewpoint of horror and awesomeness and fixation. Poe, Melville, Hawthorne, Djuna Barnes, and Julian Green in his French novels, are united in their conception of evil as being a sense of dark foreboding and the plotting of malign spirits. A dantesque or Catholic conception of evil is vastly different from that expressed in Ethan Brand or Nightwood or Le Visionnaire where evil is a tortured and introverted subjectivism. The American sense of evil comes from a special kind of fear of God which is a form of pride, and from an unwillingness to think of God as the absolute source of good which cannot be fully realized but which is at all times able to dissipate evil. I believe that the work of Henry Miller (and by work I mean his presence, his spirit, and the profoundest meaning of his books) has interrupted the traditional American treatment of evil. The obvious reason for Miller's novels not being published in America, and therefore not being accessible to the American public, is the obscenity of their language. But this violence was needed—or some comparable violence—to redirect the American consciousness of evil. The obscenity in Miller's two *Tropics* is a form of medication and catharsis, an extroversion needed after all the books of puritanical forboding. Both Miller's dissoluteness in language and his fixation on the physical possession of woman are means of liberating himself from the Hamlet-soul which has dominated the literary heroes of Europe and America during the long period between the politically unrealized revolution of 1789 and World War II.

II

"And always am I hungry," writes Henry Miller in *The Wisdom of the Heart* (p. 188). Alimentary and sexual hunger are one kind, and spiritual hunger is another. Sexual hunger is expressed in Miller's writing by means of obscenity. Because this is purely carnal, it has the savor of death and dissolution. It is a strong projection of the symbol of doom. Woman is the object of this hunger. Mr. Miller proves countless times how much more she is than the object of sexual hunger. She is a kind of test both of the reality of man and of his function. The long line of heroes extending from Hamlet to Charlie Chaplin and Donald Duck who have been awkward in the presence of woman and unable to express themselves in love, has developed in woman a false role

of dominator which D. H. Lawrence was among the first to casti-
gate. Lawrence was devoted to love, and Miller is devoted to life,
but both fear woman's role in the modern world and her usurping
of man's position. Hence their treatment of woman, in order to
undermine her role of mother for her husband and of frigid god-
dess for her lover. Lawrence treats woman as wife who is essentially mistress, and Miller treats woman as prostitute. Their use
of woman, rather than restoring her to her natural role, has become just one other perversion, comparable to man's excessive
love for his mother, as in Proust, and his excessive hate for his
mother, as in Rimbaud, a love and hate which tends to lead to
two kinds of sexual perversion.

Henry Miller knows that there is no solution to the problem
of man's sexual hunger separate from the problem of man's
spiritual hunger. He writes in his book, *The World of Sex:* "I
am essentially a religious person, and always have been" (p. 6).
Flashes everywhere in his writing testify to a sensitivity which
worships. This man is devoted in so deep a sense that his nature
has become religious. I mean by this that every action and every
word, no matter how seemingly inconsequential, have a meaning
for him and a part in the wholeness of things. The visionary is
always akin to the religious because to see the plenitude of the
cosmos is to love it and accept it. To read Henry Miller has always
been for me to discover a kind of peace in the world. He is the
one contemporary writer who has driven out from his nature
all traces of hamletism, and yet he writes constantly about Hamlet.
About Hamlet as a death-sower.

All the aspects of Miller's art and his nature are unified. He
is one person, one visionary. His vision is multiple and changing
and even contradictory. But that is as it should be. That is life.
Love is something else and Miller has defined it admirably in
The World of Sex: "Love is the drama of completion, of unification" (p. 48). The visionary is always the man able to think in
terms of mankind and to love all men as one element of the
universe. He is not always able to love individual men. The purpose of life itself attracts him more than the complexities of any
single existence. That is why he is dispensed from the usual duties
of honesty. Mr. Miller's violent attacks on Catholicism may be

explained in part by his lack of honesty in acknowledging the
effort of the Church and individuals in the Church to purify the
world. In his vision, details and debts are forgotten, and he sees
only the dark results of corruption and the blazing projects of
rejuvenation. In a recent letter to me, he writes: "Vision is the
thing. The world of the spirit is too vast and deep for mere
honesty to be of much value." (March 24, 1944.)

The love of the visionary is his vision. And God is at the end
of his vision, although not always visible, as God is in the inner-
most being of every man, although very often not discovered
there. God is always at the source, whether it be the source of
man's being, as for artists like Baudelaire and Dostoievski, or the
source of the universe, as for visionary artists like Blake, Picasso,
and Henry Miller. We are what we wish to be, what we will to
be. And we are thus for eternity. For the contemplative artist and
religious prayer is God reached. Qui non diligit manet in morte.
(I Johannis III: 14.)

FURTHER INTERPRETATIONS *

Frederick J. Hoffman

In the course of twentieth-century literary history, it has occurred to few persons simply to accept the fact of chaos and confusion, to do nothing whatsoever about it. It was more the thing to be "disillusioned," to expend much energy upon what George Orwell calls "facile despairs," and to invent new ways of interpreting the course of events, in the hope that it might be directed toward a personally conceived resolution. The negativism of dada sought on the one hand to destroy the temple; the positivism of Van Wyck Brooks, Gorham Munson and James Oppenheim sought simply to redecorate the temple, and perhaps to strengthen its supports.

Henry Miller did neither; he did not wish to destroy civilization; it was destroying itself. He certainly did not care about giving it any direction, for he allied himself with no ism, whether of the intellect or of the heart. The opening editorial of the Paris *Booster*, of which he was one of many editors, expresses well Miller's attitude. The *Booster* "has no fixed policy. It will be eclectic, flexible, alive—serious but gay withal. We will use tact and delicacy when necessary, but only when necessary. In the main the *Booster* will be a contraceptive against the self-destructive

---

* From *Freudianism and the Literary Mind*.

spirit of the age. . . . But we are fluid, quixotic, unprincipled. We have no aesthetic canons to preserve or defend." [1]

Henry Miller did not set out to explore the manifold areas and dislocations of the modern mind. His task was to accept quite without shame or indignation what he found there, and to represent it in his writings. The great, fluid sentences of his writings, their nonstop syntax and their accumulation of images obscure and obscene, these have alternately the appearance of the grandiose (Rabelaisianism without a critical or satirical purpose) and the disarmingly simple.

> As quietly and naturally as a twig falling into the Mississippi I dropped out of the stream of American life. Everything that happened to me I remember, but I have no desire to recover the past, neither have I any longings or regrets. I am like a man who awakes from a long sleep to find that he is dreaming. A pre-natal condition—the born man living unborn, the unborn man dying born. [2]

Such passivity is implicitly a criticism of the strenuous efforts of modern thinkers to find some kind of rational prop for their civilization. Miller thus belongs to the anti-intellectuals of his day; he admired Lawrence's stand against the intellectualizing of our time. Proust and Joyce, the giants of the present century, have only aggravated the modern disease by probing its sores. "This formidable picture of the world-as-disease which Proust and Joyce have given us is indeed less a picture than a microscopic study which because we see it magnified, prevents us from recognizing it as the world of every day in which we are swimming. Just as the art of psychoanalysis could not have arisen until society was sick

---

1. Editorial, *Booster*, II (1937), 5. The *Booster* had been a commercial magazine catering to American tourists in France. It changed amazingly when Miller and Co. took over. Finally, the title was changed to *Delta*.

2. Henry Miller, Selections from *Black Spring*, in *New Directions*, 1937 (Norfolk, Conn., 1937).

enough to call for this peculiar form of therapy, we could not have had a faithful image of our time until there arose in our midst monsters so ridden with disease that their works resemble the disease itself." [3]

Resignation and acceptance—they have ordinarily a religious ring. But Miller's is not the resignation of either the saint or the sinner; it is a "joyous abandonment of the will," a wish to live within the womb of time without disturbing its process. One gets closer to truth as he abandons the will, submitting to the flux of experience. Understanding is not achieved by logically reordering that experience, but by "living blissfully with it, in it, through and by it." [4] The artist who takes such a position is best able to play his proper role. He should not be a part either of the administration control of society or of the radical opposition to that control. The value of his work is that it is merely "the reflection of the automatism of life in which he is obliged to lie dormant, a sleeper on the back of sleep, waiting for the signal which will announce the moment of birth." [5]

That strange exchange of letters with Michael Fraenkel on the subject of *Hamlet* discusses, among other things, the creative process, the place of an artist in his times. In the opinion of Fraenkel, art is a means of salvation; the artist is delivered from the "aimless movement of biology." [6] Fraenkel criticizes Miller endlessly for what he calls a fear of the intellect, an unwillingness to avail himself of the mind as a source of reconstruction; he calls Miller's writing "physiological writing." Miller, says Fraenkel, is afraid to face "the man in you who stands in the same relation to you as I do, namely, Henry Miller the thinker." (157) To this accusation Miller answers that it is true the intellect is one means of communication, for the clarification and transmis-

---

3. Henry Miller, "The Universe of Death," a chapter from an unpublished book, "The World of Lawrence," in *Phoenix,* I (1938), 49.

4. Henry Miller, "Reflections on Writing," in *The Wisdom of the Heart* (Norfolk, Conn., 1941), 23.

5. Henry Miller, Selections from *The Tropic of Capricorn,* in *New Directions,* 1939 (Norfolk, Conn., 1939), 219.

6. Henry Miller and Michael Fraenkel, *Hamlet* (Santurce, Puerto Rico, 1939), [I], 46.

sion of ideas. But he is not interested in clarity as such. He has
been pleased at times to reach "those ice-cold regions of the mind,"
but the intellect is only a fortunate accident, an interruption in
the unconscious flow of man's experience and expression. More
than that, intellectualizing brings all things into doubt. To have
made a tragic figure of the doubter—so that the modern literary
scene presents a succession of two-penny Hamlets who worship
their own indecision—is one of the saddest errors of our day.
Doubt is not the end-all of thought and expression; it is not even
a proper beginning. It is merely one of the aspects of the human
psyche. "I accept Hamlet as phenomenon, just as I accept Jesus
Christ, or Krishnamurti. Passing phenomena . . . some more instructive than others." (180)

Hamlet is the archetype of the modern man, whose crippling
disease is the "thought disease." The effort to take the law unto
oneself, to make oneself the crucial moral center of the universe,
so fixed upon the self the burden of responsibility for man's collective sinning that the single self cannot well bear it. From this
source comes the "Hamlet-guilt" which plagues the modern mind
and, when projected beyond each single self, results in a babel
of conscience, moral dictates, and social panaceas. This is the "living death," the refusal to bow before the real. "Living death means
the interruption of the current of life, the forestalling of a natural
death process. It is a negative way of recognizing that the world
is really nothing but a great womb, the place where everything is
brought to life." [7] The living death is compounded of fear and
stupid optimism; the modern living death is oanistic and para-
lytic. "It's a sort of Nirvana of the Id, a condition of iceberg
without threat of thaw. This loss of contact with reality, which is
the schizophrenic motif par excellence, would be excellent if it
implied the creation of a new reality, a *poetic* reality. . . . But the
prevalent insanity is only the wolf in the cloak of the old mas-
turbative logic." [8]

Such a condition has brought a hurried call for the great spirit-

---

7. Henry Miller, "The Enormous Womb," in *Booster*, IV (1938), 21.
8. Henry Miller, "The Rise of Schizophrenia," In *New English Weekly*,
X(1936), 70.

ual healer of our day; the psychoanalyst, in Miller's opinion, ab-
solves the patient of the moral and psychic responsibility for the
world's and his own ills. This is another of the foolish illusions
by which modern man avoids both personal responsibility and the
truth: "To imagine that we are going to be saved by outside intervention, whether in the shape of an analyst, a dictator, . . . or
even God, is sheer folly." [9] As a means of testing the values of
psychoanalysis, Miller himself turned analyst in 1936. He objected
to Freud for having given to modern fears a scientific sanction;
he stands in the way of the patient's view of reality, prevents him
from accepting it. Freud is guilty of "creating a gray realism of
scientific hue instead of a Dantesque reality of black and white." [10]
Instead of revealing to the patient the chaos of the world, the
analyst seeks to cure him of it. This unfortunate circumstance prevents psychoanalysis from being the genuine and important guide
it might otherwise have been. The true analyst would "eliminate
the doctor as well as the patient, by accepting the disease itself
rather than the medicine or the mediator." (*Wisdom of the Heart*,
36)

The important contribution of psychoanalysis is its systematic
exploration of the unconscious, its service in making the unconscious a living thing, available to him who wishes to go beneath
the surface of his mind. This Miller considers a great addition, a
crucial one, to our means of salvation. But he disapproves of the
purpose to which Freud's study has been dedicated. The artist
will, if he is honest and capable, use this knowledge for another

---

9. Henry Miller, *The Wisdom of the Heart*, 35.
10. Henry Miller, "The Absolute Collective," in *The Wisdom of the
Heart*, 80. The impression Miller gives is that though he is fully informed
about psychoanalysis, and has had personal experiences as an analyst, he is
aware of its limitations and of the general failure of the analyst, to rise
above the level of commonplace figure: "They are all minor 'artists', I should
say," he writes (I assume he means by "artists," not poets or painters but
men who speak and write of problems which may be linked with the
materials of art), "and not to be compared, in lasting value with either the
poet or the religious figure." In another place in the letter he says, "I think
that some of the most egregious nonsense has been written by all the analysts.
Their worst trait is their utter humorlessness. None of them, no matter how
much they write, will ever have the effect upon the world of a Laotse."

purpose. He will find in the unconscious the real area of actual
living and dying, a place where he may hang suspended and
passive in the womb of the world. The dream-life is an important
avenue of approach. Often between the dream and reality there is
"only the thinnest line." He must withdraw, therefore, from the
analyst's bright and cheery reality, from the surface of the world,
into the unconscious. "For when, by living out his dream logic,
he fulfills himself through the destruction of his own ego, he is
incarnating for humanity the drama of individual life which to be
tasted and experienced, must embrace dissolution." (*Wisdom of
the Heart,* 8)

The final act of acceptance is expressed symbolically in terms
of the world as womb, in which man may dwell in a sort of pre-
natal security. Such dwelling among the nether regions requires
for its adequate description a style and imagery all its own, based
partly upon the functions, excretory, digestive, and sexual, references to which have been excluded most discreetly from conventional publications. It is what Fraenkel has called "physiological
writing." Miller's point of view steadfastly excludes any possibility
for a quick and easy triumph by the intellect over the unconscious sources of chaos. A new world cannot spring full-grown
from the mind of any modern Zeus. It must be passively awaited,
for implicit in chaos is the haphazard and brutal process by which
cosmic gestation takes place. The dark, forbidden processes of the
body thus gain spiritual significance by analogy with the world
as "an enormous womb." The sexual act is an unconscious process
by which forces are released which give life to the world. The
"music of the night life," is "Not heights and depths, but ecstasy
upside down, inside out, the bottom reaching as far as the top.
Abasement not just to the earth, but through the earth, through
grass and sod and subterranean stream. . . . Not the cold pricks
of conscience, nor the tormenting flagellation of the mind, but
bright, cruel blades flashing." (*Wisdom of the Heart,* 195)

Peace is thus achieved by a passive dwelling within the grotesque and obscene chaos of the world's unconscious being. Com-
menting upon the work of the painter, Hans Reichel, Miller
summarized his own attitude toward this nether reality. The great

night life of the unconscious is the source of security—not *from* but *with* pain and brutality.

> In the absolute night, in the black pain hidden away in the backbone, the substance of things is dissolved until only the essence shines forth. The objects of [Reichel's] love, as they swim up to the light to arrange themselves on his canvases, marry one another in strange mystic unions which are indissoluble. But the real ceremony goes on below, in the dark, according to the inscrutable atomic laws of wedlock. There are no witnesses, no solemn oaths. Phenomenon weds phenomenon in the way that atomic elements marry to make the miraculous substance of living matter. There are polygamous marriages and polyandrous marriages, but no morganatic marriages. There are monstrous unions too, just as in nature, and they are as inviolable, as indissoluble, as the others. Caprice rules, but it is the stern caprice of nature, and so divine.[11]

Miller accepts readily the new opportunity which psychoanalysis affords of viewing a world previously shut off from consciousness by both decorum and prudery. But his acceptance implicitly condemns the hope of psychoanalysis for a rescue of the world from its neuroses. He is, in brief, allied with no school of thought—not even with the surrealists, who seem to be burrowing in the same mine. For Miller will not grant the surrealist's assumption that personal revolution is itself a directing force. The result of all this is a peculiar form of passivity, by which means the artist becomes an organism, his writing secretions and excretions of that organism. Out of the tumult of the unconscious being come the materials for his art. Without a grasp of human tragedy or a sense of protest against the ills of the universe, he is held secure

---

11. Henry Miller, "The Cosmological Eye," in *Transition,* XXVII (1938), 323-34.

from them by the antisepsis of biological resignation. That this attitude of resignation may eventually become a part of a religious-aesthetic view of the universe is a suggestion made in a number of places in Miller's writings. For the psychoanalyst avoids the larger problem of living by using science "as a crutch"; this problem is met more directly and honestly by the poet and "the religious figure."

DEATH AND THE BAROQUE

Aldous Huxley

"The skeleton," as we all know, "was invisible in the happy days of pagan art." And invisible it remained, in spite of Christianity, for most of the centuries that followed. Throughout the Middle Ages, the knights, the mitred bishops, the ladies who warm their feet on the backs of little dogs—all are reassuringly in the flesh. No skulls adorn their tombs, no bones, no grisly reapers. Artists in words may cry, "Alas, my heart will break in three; *Terribilis mors conturbat me.*" Artists in stone are content to carve the likeness of a sleeper upon a bed. The Renaissance comes and still the sleep persists, tranquil amid the sculptured dreams of a paradise half earthly, half celestial.

> Those Pans and Nymphs ye wot of, and perchance
> Some tripod, thyrsus, with a vase or so,
> The Savior at his sermon on the mount,
> St. Praxed in a glory, and one Pan
> Ready to twitch the Nymph's last garment off,
> And Moses with the tables.

But by the middle of the sixteenth century a change has
taken place. The effigy no longer sleeps, but opens its eyes and
sits up—ideally noble, as on the Medicean tombs, or soberly a
portrait, like any one of those admirable busts in their round
niches between the pilasters of a classical design. And at the base,
below the Latin inscription, it not infrequently happens (at any
rate in Rome and after 1550) that a little skull, in bone-white
marble, reminds the onlooker of what he himself will soon be, of
what the original of the portrait has already become.

Why should the death's head have become fashionable at this
particular moment of history? The religiously minded might sur-
mise that it had something to do with the Counter-Reformation;
the medically minded, that it was connected with that sixteenth-cen-
tury pandemic of syphilis, whose noseless victims were a constant
reminder of man's latter end; the artistically minded, that some
mortuary sculptor of the time had a taste for, and a happy knack
with bones. I do not venture to decide between the possible alternatives, but am content to record the fact, observable by anyone
who has been in Rome, that there, after the middle of the century,
the skulls indubitably are.

As the years pass these reminders of mortality assume an even
greater importance. From being miniatures they grow in a short
time to full-blown, death-sized replicas of the thing behind the
face. And suddenly, imitating those bodiless seraphs of medieval
and renaissance painting they sprout a pair of wings and learn to
fly. Meanwhile the art of the late Renaissance has become the
Baroque. By an aesthetic necessity, because it is impossible for
self-conscious artists to go on doing what has been supremely well
done by their predecessors, the symmetrical gives place to the dis-
balanced, the static to the dynamic, the formalized to the realistic.
Statues are caught in the act of changing their positions; pictorial
compositions try to break out of their frames. Where there was
understatement, there is now emphasis; where there was measure
and humanity, there is now the enormous, the astounding, the
demi-god and the epileptic sub-man.

Consider, for example, those skulls on the monuments. They
have grown in size; their truth to death is overpowering and, to
heighten the effect of versimilitude, the sculptor has shifted them

from their old place on the central axis and now shows them, casual and unposed, in profile or three-quarters face, looking up to heaven or down into the grave. And their wings! Vast, wildly beating, wind-blown—the wings of vultures in a hurricane. The appetite for the inordinate grows with what it feeds upon, and along with it grow the virtuosity of the artists and the willingness of their patrons to pay for ever more astounding monuments. By 1630 the skull is no longer adequate as a memento mori; it has become necessary to represent the entire skeleton.

The most grandiose of these reminders of our mortality are the mighty skeletons which Berini made for the tombs of Urban VIII and Alexander VII in St. Peter's. Majestic in his vestments and intensely alive, each of the two Popes sits there aloft, blessing his people. Some feet below him, on either side, are his special Virtues—Faith, Temperance, Fortitude, who knows? In the middle, below the Pontiff, is the gigantic emblem of death. On Urban's tomb the skeleton is holding (slightly cock-eyed, for it would be intolerably old-fashioned and unrealistic if the thing were perfectly level) a black marble scroll inscribed with the Pope's name and title; on Alexander's the monster has been "stopped," as the photographers say, in the act of shooting up from the doorway leading into the vault. Up it comes, like a rocket, at an angle of sixty or seventy degrees, and as it rises it effortlessly lifts six or seven tons of the red marble drapery, which mitigates the rigidities or architecture and transforms the statically geometrical into something mobile and indeterminate.

The emphasis, in these two extraordinary works, is not heaven, hell, and purgatory, but on physical dissolution and the grave. The terror which inspired such works as the *Dies Irae* was of the second death, the death inflicted by an angry judge upon the sinner's soul. Here, on the contrary, the theme is the first death, the abrupt passage from animation to insensibility and from worldly glory to supper with the convocation of politic worms.

> Chi un tempo, carco d'amorose prede,
> ebbe l'ostro alle guance e l'oro al crine,
> deforme, arido teschio, ecco, si vede.

Berini's tombs are by no means unique. The Roman churches are full of cautionary skeletons. In Santa Maria sopra Minerva, for example, there is a small monument attached to one of the columns on the north side of the church. It commemorates a certain Vizzani, if I remember rightly, a jurisconsult who died some time before the middle of the seventeenth century. Here, as in the wall monuments of the High Renaissance, a bust looks out of a rounded niche placed above the long Latin catalogue of the dead man's claims upon the attention of posterity. It is the bust, so intensely lifelike as to be almost a caricature, of a florid individual in his middle forties, no fool evidently, but wearing an expression of serene and unquestioning complacency. Socially, professionally, financially, what a huge success his life had been! And how strongly, like Milton, he feels that "nothing profits more than self-esteem founded on just and right!" But suddenly we become aware that the bust in its round frame is being held in an almost amorous embrace by a great skeleton in high relief, whizzing diagonally, from left to right, across the monument. The lawyer and all his achievements, all his self-satisfaction, are being wafted away into darkness and oblivion.

Of the same kind, but still more astounding, are the tombs of the Pallavicino family in San Francesco a Ripa. Executed by Mazzuoli at the beginning of the eighteenth century, these monuments are among the last and at the same time the most extravagant outflowerings of the baroque spirit. Admirably carved, the usual Virtues keep guard at the base of each of the vast pyramidal structures. Above them, flapping huge winds, a ten-foot skeleton in bronze holds up for our inspection a pair of oval frames, containing busts of the departed Pallavicini. On one side of the family chapel we see the likenesses of two princely ecclesiastics. Death holds them with a studied carelessness, tilting their frames a little, one to the left, the other to the right, so that the grave ascetic faces look out, as though through the ports of a rolling ship. Opposite them, in the hands of another and, if possible, even more frightful skeleton, are two more members of the family—an elderly princess, this time, and her spouse. And what a spouse! Under the majestic wig the face is gross, many-chinned, complacently imbecile. High blood pressure inflates the whole squat person almost to bursting point; pride keeps the pig-snout chronically pointing to the skies. And it is Death who now holds him aloft; it is Corruption who, with triumphant derision, exhibits him, forever pilloried in marble, a grotesque and pitiable example of human bumptiousness.

Looking at the little fat man up there in the skeleton's clutches, one reflects with a certain astonishment, that some Pallavicino must have ordered and presumably paid for this strange monument to a departed relative. With what intentions? To display the absurdity of the old gentleman's pretensions to grandeur? To make a mock of everything he had lived for? The answer to these questions is, at least in part, affirmative. All these baroque tombs were doctrinally sound. The heirs of popes and princes laid out huge sums to celebrate the glories of their distinguished forebears—but laid them out on monuments whose emphatically Christian theme is the transience of earthly greatness and the vanity of human wishes. After which they addressed themselves with redoubled energy to the task of satisfying their own cravings for money, position, and power. A belief in hell and the knowledge that every ambition is doomed to frustration at the hands of a skeleton have never prevented the majority of human beings from behaving as though death were no more than an unfounded rumor and survival, a thing beyond the bounds of possibility. The men of the Baroque differed from those of other epochs not in what they actually did, not even in what they thought about those doings, but in what they were ready to express of their thoughts. They liked an art that harps on death and corruption and were neither better or worse than we who are reticent about such things.

The fantastic dance of death in San Francesco a Ripa is almost the last of its kind. Thirty years after it was carved, Robert Blair could achieve a modest popularity by writing such lines as these:

> Methinks I see thee with thy head low
>   laid,
> While surfeited upon thy damask cheek

The high-fed worm, in lazy volumes
    rolled,
Riots unscared.

But eighteenth-century sculptors made no attempt to realize
these gruesome images. On graves and monuments Death no
longer comments upon the mad pretensions of his victims. Broken
columns, extinguished torches, weeping angels and muses—these
are now the emblems in vogue. The artist and his patron are
concerned to evoke sentiments less painful than the horror of
corruption. With the nineteenth century we enter an age of
stylistic revivals; but there is never a return to the mortuary fash-
ions of the Baroque. From the time of Mazzuoli until the present
day no monument to any important European has been adorned
with death's heads or skeletons.

We live habitually on at least three levels—the level of
strictly individual existence, the level of intellectual abstraction,
and the level of historical necessity and social convention. On the
first of these levels our life is completely private; on the others it
is, at least partially, a shared and public life. Thus, writing about
death, I am on the level of intellectual abstraction. Participating
in the life of a generation to which the mortuary art of the
Baroque seems odd and alien, I am on the level of history. But
when I actually come to die, I shall be on the first level, the level
of exclusively individual experience. That which, in human life,
is shared and public has always been regarded as more respectable
than that which is private. Kings have their Astronomers Royal,
emperors their official Historiographers; but there are no Royal
Gastronomers, no Papal or Imperial Pornographers. Among
crimes, the social and historical are condoned as the last infirmities
of a noble mind, and their perpetrators are very generally admired.
The lustful and intemperate, on the contrary, are condemned by
all—even by themselves (which was why Jesus so much preferred
them to the respectable Pharisees). We have no God of Brothels,
but the God of Battles, alas, is still going strong.

Baroque mortuary sculpture has as its basic subject matter

the conflict on one important front, between the public and the private, between the social and the individual, between the historical and the existential. The prince in his curly wig, the Pope in his vestments, the lawyer with his Latin eulogy and his smirk of self-satisfaction—all these are pillars of society, representatives of great historical forces and even makers of history. But under smirk and wig and tiara is the body with its unshareable physiological processes, is the psyche with its insights and sudden graces, its abysmal imbecilities and its unavowable desires. Every public figure—and to some extent we are all public figures—is also an island universe of private experiences; and the most private of all these experiences is that of falling out of history, of being separated from society—in a word, the experience of death.

Based as they always are upon ignorance—invincible in some cases, voluntary and selective in others—historical generalizations can never be more than partially true. In spite of which and at the risk of distorting the facts to fit a theory, I would suggest that, at any given period, preoccupation with death is in inverse ratio to the prevalence of a belief in man's perfectibility through and in a properly organized society. In the art and literature of the age of Condorcet, of the age of Herbert Spencer and Karl Marx, of the age of Lenin and the Webbs there are few skeletons. Why? Because it was during the eighteenth and nineteenth centuries that men came to believe in progress, in the march of history toward an even bigger and better future, in salvation, not for the individual, but for society. The emphasis is on history and environment, which are regarded as the primary determinants of individual destiny. Indeed, among orthodox Marxians they are now (since the canonization of Lysenko and the anathema pronounced on "reactionary Morganism") regarded as the sole determinants. Predestination, whether Augustinian or Mendelian, whether *karmic* or genetic, has been ruled out, and we are back with Helvetius and his shepherd boys who can all be transformed into Newtons, back with Dr. Watson and his infinitely conditionable infants. But meanwhile the fact remains that, in this still unregenerate world, each of us inherits a physique and a temperament. Moreover the career of every individual man or woman is essentially non-progressive. We reach maturity only to decline into decriptude and the body's death. Could anything be more painfully obvious? And yet how rarely in the course of the past two hundred and fifty years has death been made the theme of any considerable work of art! Among the great painters only Goya has chosen to treat of death, and then only of death by violence, death in war. The mortuary sculptors, as we have seen, harp only on the sentiments surrounding death—sentiments ranging from the noble to the tender and even the voluptuous. (The most delicious buttocks in the whole repertory of art are to be found on Canova's monument to the last of the Stuarts.)

In the literature of this same period death has been handled more frequently than in painting or scultpre, but only once (to my knowledge, at least) with complete adequacy. Tolstoy's *The Death of Ivan Ilyitch* is one of the artistically most perfect and at the same time one of the most terrible books ever written. It is the story of an utterly commonplace man who is compelled to discover, step by agonizing step, that the public personage with whom, all his life, he has identified himself is hardly more than a figment of the collective imagination, and that his essential self is the solitary, insulated being who falls sick and suffers, rejects and is rejected by the world and finally (for the story has a happy ending) gives in to his destiny and in the act of surrender, at the very moment of death, finds himself alone and naked in the presence of the Light. The baroque sculptors are concerned with the same theme but they protest too much and their conscious striving for sublimity is apt to defeat its own object. Tolstoy is never emphatic, indulges in no rhetorical flourishes, speaks simply of the most difficult matters and flatly, matter-of-factly of the most terrible. That is why his book has such power and is so profoundly disturbing to our habitual complacency. We are shocked by it in much the same way we are shocked by pornography—and for the same reason. Sex is almost as completely private a matter as death, and a work of art which powerfully expresses the truth about either of them is very painful to the respectable public figure we imagine ourselves to be. Nobody can have the consolations of religion or philosophy unless he has first experienced their desolations. And nothing is more desolating than a thorough knowledge of the private self. Hence the utility of such books as *Ivan Ilyitch* and, I would venture to add, such books as Henry Miller's *Tropic of Cancer*.

And here let me add a parenthetical note on the pornography of the age which witnessed the rise of the ideas of progress and social salvation. Most of it is merely pretty, an affair of wish-fulfillments—Boucher carried to his logical conclusion. The most celebrated pornographer of the time, the Marquis de Sade, is a mixture of escapist maniac and *philosophe*. He lives in a world where insane phantasy alternates with post-Voltairean ratiocination; where impossible orgies are interrupted in order that the participants may talk, sometimes shrewdly, but more often in the shallowest eighteenth-century way, about morals, politics, and metaphysics. Here, for example, is a typical specimen of Sadian sociology. "Is incest dangerous? Certainly not. It extends family ties and consequently renders more active the citizen's love of his fatherland." In this passage, as throughout the work of this oddest product of the Enlightenment, we see the public figure doing his silly best to rationalize the essentially unrationalizable facts of private existence. But what we need, if we are to know ourselves, is the truthful and penetrating expression in art of precisely these unrationalizable facts—the facts of death, as in *Ivan Ilyitch*, the facts of sex, as in *Tropic of Cancer*, the facts of pain and cruelty, as in Goya's "Disasters," the acts of fear and disgust and fatigue, as in that most horrifyingly truthful of war-books, *The Naked and the Dead*. Ignorance is a bliss we can never afford; but to know only ourselves is not enough. If it is to be a fruitful desolation, self-knowledge must be made the road to a knowledge of the Other. Unmitigated, it is but another form of ignorance and can lead only to despair or complacent cynicism. Floundering between time and eternity, we are amphibians and must accept the fact. *Noverim me, noverim Te* the prayer expresses an essentially realistic attitude towards the universe in which, willy-nilly, we have to live and to die.

III

Death is not the only private experience with which baroque
art concerns itself. A few yards away from the Pallavicino tombs
reclines Bernini's statue of Blessed Ludovica Albertoni in ecstasy. Here, as in the case of the same artist's more celebrated St.
Teresa, the experience recorded is of a privacy so special that, at
a first glance, the spectator feels a shock of embarrassment. Entering those rich chapels in San Franscesco and Sanata Maria della
Vittoria, one has the impression of having opened a bedroom
door at the most inopportune of moments, almost of having opened
The Tropic of Cancer at one of its most startling pages. The posture of the ecstatics, their expression and the exuberance of the
tripe-like drapery which surrounds them and, in the Albertoni's
case, overflows in a kind of peritoneal cataract onto the altar below—all conspire to emphasize the fact that, though saints may
be important historical figures, their philosophy is as disquietingly
private as anyone else's.

By the inner logic of the tradition within which they worked,
baroque artists were committed to a systematic exploitation of the
inordinate. Hence the epileptic behavior of their gesticulating or
swooning personages, and hence, also, their failure to find an adequate artistic expression for the mystical experience. This failure
seems all the more surprising when one remembers that their
period witnessed a great efforescence of mystical religion. It was
the age of St. John of the Cross and Benet of Canfield, of Mme.
Acarie and Father Lallemant and Charles de Condren, of Augus-
tine Baker and Surin and Olier.

All these had taught that the end of the spiritual life is the
unitive knowledge of God, an immediate intuition of Him beyond
discursive reason, beyond imagination, beyond emotion. And all
had insisted that visions, raptures, and miracles were not the "real
thing," but mere by-products which, if taken too seriously, could
become fatal impediments to spiritual progress. But visions, raptures, and miracles are astounding and picturesque occurrences;
and astounding and picturesque occurrences were the predestined

subject matter of artists whose concern was with the inordinate. In baroque art the mystic is represented either as a psychic with supernormal powers, or as an ecstatic, who passes out of history in order to be alone, not with God, but with his or her physiology in a state hardly distinguishable from that of sexual enjoyment. And this in spite of what all the contemporary masters of the spiritual life were saying about the dangers of precisely this sort of thing.

Such a misinterpretation of mysticism was made inevitable by the very nature of baroque art. Given the style in which they worked, the artists of the seventeenth century could not have treated the theme in any other way. And oddly enough, even at times when the current style permitted a treatment of the less epileptic aspects of religion, no fully adequate rendering of the contemplative life was ever achieved in the plastic arts of Christendom. The peace that passes all understanding was often sung and spoken; it was hardly ever painted or carved. Thus, in the writings of St. Bernard, of Albertus Magnus, of Eckhart and Tauler and Ruysbroeck one may find passages that express very clearly the nature and significance of mystical contemplation. But the saints who figure in medieval painting and sculpture tell us next to nothing about this anticipation of beatific vision. There are no equivalents of those Far Eastern Buddhas and Bodhisattvas who incarnate, in stone and paint, the experience of ultimate reality. Moreover the Christian saints have their being in a world from which non-human Nature (that mine of supernatural beauties and transcendent significances) has been almost completely excluded. In his handbook on painting Cennini gives a recipe for mountains. Take some large jagged stones, arrange them on a table, draw them and, lo and behold, you will have a range of Alps or Appennines good enough for all the practical purposes of art. In China and Japan mountains were taken more seriously. The aspiring artist was advised to go and live among them, to make himself alertly passive in their presence, to contemplate them lovingly until he could understand the mode of their being and feel within them the working of the immanent and transcendent Tao. As one might have expected, the medieval artists of Christendom painted mere backgrounds, whereas those of the Far East

painted landscapes that are the equivalent of mystical poetry—
formally perfect renderings of man's experience of being related
to the Order of Things.

   This experience is, of course, perfectly private, non-historical,
and unsocial. That is why, to the organizers of churches and the
exponents of salvation through the state, it has always seemed to
be suspect, shady, and even indecent. And yet, like sex and pain
and death, there it remains one of the brute facts with which,
whether we like them or not, we have to come to terms. Madden-
ingly, unbearably, an occasional artist rubs our noses in his rendering of these facts. Confronted by the pornographies of suffering, of sensuality, of dissolution, by "The Disasters of War" and
The Naked and the Dead, by *Tropic of Cancer,* by *Ivan Ilyitch*
and even (despite their ludicrous sublimity) by the baroque tombs,
we shrink and are appalled. And in another way there is something hardly less appalling in the pornographies (as many good
rationalists regard them) of mysticism. Even the consolations of
religion and philosophy are pretty desolating for the average sensual man, who clings to his ignorance as the sole guarantee of
happiness. *Terribilis mors conturbat me;* but so does *terribilis
Vita.*

The Fifties

Perhaps it is the repeated appeal to "culture" which gives Alwyn Lee's essay its representative flavor. The tone makes it clear that it is not merely the "dwindling capital of the Christian tradition" which concerns Lee, but its total bankruptcy, at least if Miller and some other "artist-hermits" are to be taken as representative. That, however, is precisely Mr. Lee's point. Miller is not, cannot be, representative of anything except a radical deracination, a pathological isolation brilliantly if horribly illustrating the all too pervasive "cruel and clumsy fun this century has played with the mind."

While we may find ourselves short of patience with the obvious commitments underlying Lee's point of view, we need to be reminded that the perspective which the reader of the seventies brings to this article is likely to prove of dubious advantage. For while something of the aesthetic conservatism, the nostalgia for passing, or past, values pervades the essay, its main point is difficult to contest. A total cultural isolation is an impossibility, and there is something of the monstrous and pathetic in those who pretend to such an isolation. The question is whether Miller's isolation, if that is what it is, is precisely "cultural." Moreover, granting the basic unwieldliness of all definitions, is there not such a cultural lag (regardless of who is separated from whom) in the relationship between virtually all artists and their societies? At the very least, Lee's position is a provocative counter to that of Wallace Fowlie, and an interesting representative of an historical period characterized in large part by retrenchment.

Of the many who have been moved to pay unabashed tribute to Miller, Karl Shapiro is one of the few who has done so by a method other than denigrating the persons and principals of those of a different persuasion. Despite the fact that he considers Miller "The Greatest Living Author," Shapiro candidly admits that a catalog of the influential books in Miller's life reads like a "period list"; and agrees that Miller is "no writer" if Henry James represents the standard for judgment. Moreover, he acknowledges that in terms of literary history, Miller's views are by no means unique, although they are atypical, as were those of Whitman and Thoreau. Indeed, it is "his time and place" which give Miller his particular distinction in Shapiro's eyes because "he is the only American of our time who has given us a full-scale interpretation of modern America." He is the only American author who is applying "cosmic consciousness" to the silent generation.

Although hardly an apologist for "The Beats," Shapiro clearly shared with them, and with Miller, a profound alienation from modern America. For this reason his observations on Miller's significance take on particular relevance in light of the movement of the disaffected young from the marginal Beats to the Hippies, and now the Yippies. It is Miller's particular and characteristic existential posture, his literary life style, which interests Shapiro. In one sense Shapiro is not engaged here in literary criticism at all. He is untroubled by the admission that "as a writer Miller may be second- or third-rate or of no rating at all" because it is as a man-in-the-world, as a "spiritual example," that Miller has his chief significance.

Thus Shapiro's essay is the complement to Orwell's. Neither of them are primarily concerned with Miller as an artist *qua* artist, as a writer employing symbols or a point of view, as an artist with a "style." Yet they differ fundamentally on what this artist as exemplar exemplifies, because they differ on what man as artist *ought* to concern himself with. And if the quarrel is never ending, it is worth recalling that the choice, for reader and writer alike, is equally so.

Frank Kermode comes directly to grips with the subject of his essay: the relationship, or lack of it, between Miller and the critics. Kermode urges that the task of the critic is to acquire a firm grip on an author's work without himself appearing to identify himself necessarily with the author's view of literature. To achieve this end, the critic is obliged to go about his proper business, which is to assess a writer's significance in light of the tradition to which he belongs. Kermode then proceeds to demonstrate the very real contribution that criticism so conceived can make, particularly to a writer such as Miller to whom critics and criticism are anything but congenial.

"The critic can at least say what is commonplace in Miller's anti-literature." As Kermode observes, there is much that is conventional, which is to say, having a literary heritage, in Miller's work. The bohemian life in the corrupt metropolis; Miller's anti-intellectualism; repudiation of objective/abstract thought, with the attendant predilection for chronological primitivism and fascination with the occult—all of these and more are evidence of Miller's ties to "the big nineteenth century myth." Kermode's presentation is a model of brevity and precision. Moreover, his defense of criticism in the employment of its procedures is as persuasive as it is informative.

But, as he acknowledges, a survey of the conventional elements in a writer's work has no very direct bearing upon his quality as a writer. Indeed, when it comes to quality, it is difficult to know how Kermode's commitments to form and *mesure* are intrinsically better than commitments to their opposites. In such pristine purity that is not, however, the point. Kermode urges refusal of the invitation to make a random choice among exclusive alternatives. The advantage that knowledge of a literary heritage bequeaths is that while in the process of choosing our values, we may succeed in avoiding the temptation to choose them on the basis of attributes which individual works either do not possess, or possess only at second hand.

HENRY MILLER—THE PATHOLOGY
OF ISOLATION

Alwyn Lee

Rebecca West once found a quality common to Yeats, Kipling and George Moore: "They knew nothing of life they had not found out for themselves." Temperament and circumstances of quasicolonial birth had deprived them of organic identity with their own culture so that they always wrote somewhat as strangers —from the outside looking in. Each was insulated from the general sense of their time and place in such a way that they developed unpredictable eccentricities and vulgarities involving taste and belief. It took a keen, if not arrogant nose to detect that these three traditional writers were provincials of their own tradition— "outsiders" as the English used to say; but it needs no special insight to note the appearance in this generation of something much more extreme. This is the artist-hermit whose subject matter is his own isolation and singularity.

The hermits are gregarious. Entire little magazines such as *Partisan Review* seem given over to this glum preoccupation of the contributors with their own condition—the artist's alienation, deracination, sickness, etc. It suggests the dilemma of the infant who cannot make the bridge between the desire to express and the need to communicate. In fact, the problems of infancy do loom large; the "artists" are busy following the spoor of their undoing back to the diaper and beyond.

The problem child of this strange avant-garde is Henry Miller. He is perhaps its purest exemplar though not its ablest exponent, for only this special generation could have produced in Henry Miller a true *naif,* born yesterday, for whom nothing is a *given,* for whom (to refer to Miss West) everything he knows is a discovery of his own.

He is perhaps the first *total* proletarian—one who is proletarianized *in time,* whose cultural equipment, like a hobo's gear, consists of oddments queerly perverted from their original use. Miller is thus important as a symbol of how deep a fissure has grown between our culture and its own origins, of how this century may exclude those apparently living in its midst, of what (with purely local literary matters in view) Lionel Trilling called "the persistent discontinuity of our culture." Lenin sneered at those who wished merely to understand rather than change history. As a total proletarian, deprived of real property in the past, Miller once proposed to abolish it.

He recalls that "I used to write that memory must be killed off, that if the intervals between births and deaths had any purpose, it must be to get rid of the baggage of memory." This has the logic of lunacy; it is the mind hankering after the pure condition of anarchy with each element of the blooming buzzing confusion cut off from meaning in the unbridgeable instants of an Eleatic time. It is an insupportable position, and to it belongs Miller's surrealist exercises, where, with a cast and properties of furred batrachians, libidinous wallpaper, atrocious tomcats and what not, a gesture is made toward absolute irrelevance and discontinuity. Of course, it could never be more than a gesture, but this is one of the things Miller has had to find out for himself. Indeed, it is the legitimate fruit of his courage and the measure of his talents that what he *has* found out amounts to so much, though inevitably his findings make an odd compilation.

With the touchingly unlucky eclecticism of looting soldiery, Miller has peopled his private world with Blake and Madame Blavatsky, Rimbaud and Abe Rattner, Buddha and Anaïs Nin, Christ and Swami Vivekananda. He is also happy to have found a number of acquaintances of great genius: all comprise an ill-paired arkful of cultural livestock. The erratic whims of its Noah are usually put down to mere willfulness or exhibitionism—the pranks of an aging *enfant terrible;* but much more is involved. These are the heroic frenzies of a fatally isolated man trying to construct about himself a one-man culture. It is the fate of a man who has rejected traditional religion as "s—t" and is obliged to invent his own; who has rejected society and founds a colony. What concerns us here is that Miller, having rejected most traditional literature, feels moved to write his own. "Men no longer communicate," he announces. "That is the tragedy of modern times. Society has long since ceased to be a community; it has broken up into aggregations of helpless atoms." It is, however, not Miller's role to explain or repair this matter, but to exemplify it. An involuntary solipsist, all his writings whether loosely called fiction, philosophy, criticism or politics are so many forms of autobiography—episodes in an endless anecdote.

Thus, when Miller is explicitly autobiographical, he is at his best—a wonderful, spirited and scandalous raconteur in the books where he has established the reputation he squanders in matters of which he knows nothing. In *Tropic of Capricorn* and *Tropic of Cancer,* his creatures gambol weightlessly in the present tense. In one of the *Tropics,* I forget which, Miller makes not the usual disclaimer that his characters bear no resemblance to any living person, but that they are, in fact, dead. This sort of thing is of fairly long standing in "modern" writing, its first appearance was perhaps *The Young European,* published after the First World War in, of course, *Transition,* but for a while at least, Miller found this bleak climate very bracing.

For most writers, "I" is an ambiguous protean affair upon which many claims are staked—by God, the family or the state, but none of the embarrassment of the personal pronoun clings to Miller. In anecdote, he has the tactical advantages of an invisible man or a messenger from Mars (who unaccountably wears a Western Union uniform.) When he tries to deal in general ideas, the boot is on the other foot: Miller is all too plainly visible, but he can see nothing. It is only when he writes, not from within his isolation but about its origins (as in "'The Tailor Shop," his best story) that he is able to touch others. Then he becomes a moving figure with the "attractiveness" (as he writes of someone else) "of a man about to go insane."

Miller was born in Brooklyn, symbolically a foundling, on the doorstep of New York. The first voice to touch an echo in his nature was that of Emma Goldman. It was probably not anarchism-as-politics which is a humorless and boring thing, but anarchism as a private and secular eschatology which reached Miller. After anarchism of a sort, there followed exemption from the war, and then that general exemption—exile. Miller's exile was something special. Those of the lost generation (Hemingway, Fitzgerald, Cowley, etc.) were mere truants, who, despite bull fights, the Ritz or the Left Bank remained as American as Dodsworth-not-yet-returned natives enjoying a temporary expatriation. But Miller, a true waif, achieved exile without nostalgia, which Santayana, who ought to know, says is a bad thing. Miller's exile was a dramatic form of an inner condition; consider it by contrast with the easy transplantations of those well-potted growths—T. S. Eliot or Henry James. In the United States, Miller remains rootless—an internal exile—able, in *The Air-Conditioned Nightmare*, to see his country with a tourist's eye.

In France, he believed he saw a different state of affairs—a homogeneous culture and a tradition strong enough "to make even its atheists catholic." But a tradition is not to be adopted; those old clothes will never fit. Nor would England do. Early, Miller wrestled English culture (in the person of an incomprehensible policeman) to a fall, and since that encounter, more comic than Miller seemed to know, he has had no time for that tradition-clogged island, except for its production of gnostic Blake.[1] Until he went to Greece, where Delphic practices, it seems, still flourish, Miller did not find any place in which he felt at home.

---

1. In this matter, Miller shows himself again a true, if unacknowledged exemplar of the avant-garde. For some reason the very idea of a parent culture sets up an uncontrollable irritation in the breast of a progressive writer, suggesting that Anglophobia is the anti-Semitism of the Left. Randolph Bourne has been perhaps the funniest contributor to this literature, although Edmund Wilson, veteran bellwether of trends, has been certainly the most irritable.

Meanwhile, he had been gripped by a more appropriate, very private idea of an obsessive kind—the myth of the vagabond god. He had discovered Rimbaud.

In the Education of Henry Miller (a highly progressive affair!) the discovery of Rimbaud was a decisive, if somewhat mysterious matter. As Miller tells it, he "surrendered" to Rimbaud "after reading a few lines . . . and trembling like a leaf put the book away." Yet this was at a time when Miller tells us he knew virtually no French. There is a bi-lingual *Saison d'Enfer* but that was not it. Evidently something peculiar happened. Unless some new kind of communication was involved (and Miller in his more vatic moments is not above suggesting things of this kind) it could not have been the poetry, but the myth, Rimbaud at Harar, the god-like prodigal, which confronted Miller from the half-understood words and entranced him. "In Rimbaud, I see myself as in a mirror." Much of Miller's career can be seen as an elaboration of this identification fantasy.

Can sanity be won by rejection of an insane world? Or innocence achieved by rejection of our guilty involvement in history's plot against us? Should a new world be made of new things? This, no less, is Miller's huge presumption. In terms of it he has been willing to make of himself a completely private person, or as the Greeks had it, an idiot. Deracination of this degree is a new thing in history. In so far as it has expressed itself in surrealism, it has been identified by Cyril Connolly as "a typical city-delirium movement." Some debacle of the intelligence is involved. It suggests that the wild and irrelevant volubility of these *"paysans de Paris"* is a modern counterpart of the mute idiocy of the clod-headed peasant with which other ages are reproached. The Man With The Hoe leers across history at his brother in deprivation— The Man With The Soft Watch. No doubt the smug hindsight of future scholars will find a term (probably theological) for the fragmentation of the twentieth century mind. Meanwhile, let us try a metaphor from science.

Spiritually, we are all hard of hearing, but we get along somehow. Miller's lurching mind suggests the radical sort of deafness of those whose inner ear is destroyed. Such people must keep their balance by visual means; in the dark they topple and floun-

der as if they had never learned to walk. Miller's wild vagaries of
judgment in which acute perception alternates with illiterate
piffle suggests some such radical defect, the absence of some os-
motic faculty that should give him touch with the order of living
things and the things other men know and have known. Whatever
condition isolates Miller it is his value that he announces it. *"Je
est un autre,"* says Rimbaud-Miller ("I" has become a thing) and
Miller-Rimbaud knows what to blame: "For the anarchy of society
the artist answers with anaudia." In other words if reality makes
hateful and incomprehensible noises, there is always shellshock.

However, the non-artist is invited to listen to the noises which
come from within the silence, and must try to make what he can
of them. This is not rewarding work now that Miller has abandoned the story in favor of tracts, exhortations, jottings, notes,
asides, conversations, etc. Unhappily also, this non-stop diary often
puts Miller in a field where the huge claims he makes for the
quasi-divine status of the artist founder on items of what used to
be called common knowledge; alternatively, he offers some basic
theorem of existence as if he were its Pythagoras.

In one of his recent illuminations Miller discovered that, after
all, memory has a place in life; we cannot disengage ourselves
from our own past. The discovery was exciting enough to provide
the title for the book—*Remember to Remember;* and Miller announced this commonplace axiom of the human condition, this
thing that everyone else always knew, with an engaging air of
originality reminiscent only of the hermit who emerged from his
cave to release the news that after thirty years' meditation he had
invented the wheel.

At least, it might be claimed that life within the private
mind is not dull. Let those who have a taste for such quarry stalk
a few exotic specimens which have been added to Miller's well-
stocked preserve of fearsome game. Here is one which might possibly be the result of the mating of Bernard Shaw (of the preface
to *Back to Methuselah*) and Annie Besant (of *The Secret Wisdom*): "When the desire to be in a distant place becomes greater
than the physical means of getting there, we will certainly discover how to be in that place without the means of a conveyance."
(Is it a plane? Is it a bird? Is it a man? Why it's Henry Miller!)

Here is another in which he annuonces the creation of the drama. This futurist madness is one antithetical to the folly of scholars and critics which aspires to the definitive, which attempts to say the last word. Miller is actually involved in an attempt to say the first word. Miller has never written on the theater (that is, if charity exempts some witless horseplay at the expense of *Hamlet*), yet he has only to write a few sentences about a repertory group in Moylan, Pennsylvania, before he has abolished all other and previous theater—dramatists and all. "If the theater became alive [like this] . . . it would not need plays already written out, it would improvise, it would act out events spontaneously . . ." etc.

Miller has discovered a number of geniuses whose work, as described by Miller, resembles nothing ever seen on land or sea unless perhaps his own. Miller confers upon them all (including one whose work, he cheerfully admits, is "atrociously bad," though, of course, "rich and exalted") his own militant sense of vocation. Alas, there has been only one Rimbaud, but Miller keeps hearing voices calling from coteries from Monterey to Manhattan, and belligerently tells one and all that only a dirty culture-snob would question their coherence. In Miller's world, it is the vocation—the artist's vocation, that is—which is important, not its outcome. Kathleen Raine has mentioned somewhere that the modern artist's studio had come to acquire some of the prestige that once belonged to the monk's cell. If that is so, it implies that criticizing an artist is rather like heckling a beadsman at his pieties. Miller certainly seems to hold that view, and with it, a new definition of art as what artists do. Hence his savage defense of the sacred artist-piffler [2] against the profane critic ("Hired prostitute") and his inability to distinguish between art and piffle because both issue from the same sacred source.

There are political thickets in the Miller canebrakes, but we must push on through these, only remarking a similarity of tone with the cranky politics of Céline (though Miller is no anti-

---

2. Wyndham Lewis did up a coterie of such in *The Apes of God*, notably with Dan, the moron-pansy-genius, but, so much for the power of satire, there are now whole suburbs full.

Semite), a writer with whom he has strong affinities. No one would bother to make a political case against Miller, for here, as in other general ideas, Miller's isolation condemns him to be merely the historian—indeed the choreographer—of his own attitudes.

Miller's one-man culture, like a one-man band, has demanded ingenuity and energy and the din has been terrific. The ears of the sensitive are stunned but something is becoming clear amid the uproar. Miller's lumpish philosophizings continue to astound the logician, but Miller himself as an exemplary personage is becoming more explicit—a well-rounded figure of the cruel and clumsy fun this century has played with the mind. He has become quite a character.

In his Western migration Miller has added another sure touch to that gaudy invention, his life—a tragi-comic work of art of which his writings are the mere program notes. Miller has arrived at his Harar; the climate is wonderful and the natives have proved more than friendly. A word about these natives and Miller's prestige among them. We are all living on the dwindling capital of the Christian tradition that produced us; our intellectual economy has become antiquarian; like Europeans we grub for our household gods amid the rubble. Some have repudiated the unequal struggle, lapsed into a low food-gatherers' economy. Among these intellectually displaced persons flourishes Miller's black market in ideas. There is a thoroughly modern rightness about Miller's mind, a surrealist quality like a perambulator full of loot—the rare and delicate heirloom equated with the kilogram of frostbitten tubers—suggesting the symbol of a general debacle. The fact is that the "bursting asunder of the social integument" of which Marx spoke has taken place, though not in the manner he predicted. "When all that was sacred has been profaned . . . and all that was solid melts in air . . ." it was promised that man would face his "true condition" with "sober senses." It was the eminent prophet's worst prediction. On the contrary no one's senses are quite sober. There is hell to pay in the Western world's big progressive school. As the fabric of Christian culture shreds away, aberrations of mind and belief (once private disasters) become sizable social phenomena. There is a mild and wacky form of this general distress and for some reason the West Coast is the place for this sort of thing. There, the well-fed orphans of Western culture build their cosy private asylums; these are the sun-tanned, sexually-limber nihilists, devotees of swamis and neighborhood religions, customers of deep-enema temples, dianetics men, food cranks and astrologists who make up the notorious personnel of what Southern California politicians call the "chiropractic vote." There is a more or less literate sector of this franchise and it is Miller's fatality to have cornered it. He has become the Principal Person of the Miller Cult. To be sure, Miller protests at this talk of a cult (he blames the English for starting it, of all people) but no one who has permitted publication of a multicolored brochure of "homage" to himself is in any shape to cough modestly at this stage. It was an appropriate outcome and there are signs that Miller is astute enough to know this. At all events he has bloomed in the goofy ambience of the coastal colony, his pronouncements are received as those of a *guru* and a kindly avuncular gruffness begins to overlay the forensic manner. Soon, he may be no angrier than Philip Wylie. Perhaps as a symptom of this emollient process, those four-letter words that made the *Tropics* popular G.I. souvenirs of Paris are becoming scarcer. Evidently Miller has decided, more or less like another prudent Henry, that Boston is worth an asterisk.

Like other regions to which we are assured the far future belongs, California now seems to live in the near past. There flowers again the revolutionary simpleton and the bohemian romanticism of Greenwich Village of the twenties. This time lag extends even to costume, and Miller dotes on every glass bead of it. At least they seem to be glass beads . . . "Virginia is trying on her new gown made of dyed hemp and studded with Indra's thousand eyes all a twinkle. . . ."

These foolish and dreary goings on would hardly be worth looking into unless larger things were involved. Miller is able to state his own and others' predicament; "Men no longer communicate." As to what can restore community between men, Miller (surprisingly for one able to say that what comes from official pulpits is s—t) asserts: "Only the presence and worship of God." This may very well be true and the crux of the whole matter, but there is the uneasy reflection that Miller may think to have some spectacular hand in it. There was the soothsayer in Greece by whom Miller was assured that he would be taken straight up to heaven (from Tibet was it?), after many wonderful events. There are other disquieting symptoms on record. Miller coyly recalls that in translating Rimbaud, he once read "il" for "Dieu." Considering the nature of his identification with Rimbaud this is a Freudian *lapsis* of unprecedented dimensions—surely the first time anyone has conferred divinity upon himself by a slip of the typewriter.

THE GREATEST LIVING AUTHOR:
IN DEFENSE OF IGNORANCE

Karl Shapiro

How is one to talk about Miller? There are authors one cannot write a book or even a good essay about. Arthur Rimbaud is one (and Miller's book on Rimbaud is one of the best books on Rimbaud ever written, although it is mostly about Henry Miller). D. H. Lawrence is another author one cannot encompass in a book "about" (Miller abandoned his book on Lawrence). And Miller himself is one of those Patagonian authors who just won't fit into a book. Every word he has ever written is autobiographical, but only in the way *Leaves of Grass* is autobiographical. There is not a word of "confession" in Miller. His amorous exploits are sometimes read as a kind of Brooklyn Casanova or male Fanny Hill, but there is probably not a word of exaggeration or boasting to speak of—or only as much as the occasion would call for. The reader can and cannot reconstruct the life of Henry Miller from his books, for Miller never sticks to the subject any more than Lawrence does. The fact is that there isn't any subject and Miller is its poet. But a little information about him might help present him to those who need an introduction. For myself, I do not read him consecutively; I choose one of his books blindly and open it at random. I have just done this; for an example, I find: "Man is not at home in the universe, despite all the efforts of philosophers and metaphysicians to provide a soothing syrup. Thought is still a narcotic. The deepest question is *why*. And it is a forbidden one. The very asking is in the nature of cosmic sabotage. And the penalty is—the afflictions of Job." Not the greatest prose probably, but Miller is not a writer; Henry James is a writer. Miller is a talker, a streetcorner gabbler, a prophet, and a Patagonian.

What is this "acceptance" Orwell mentions in regard to Whitman and Henry Miller? On one level it is the poetry of cosmic consciousness, and on the most obvious level it is the poetry of the Romantic nineteenth century. Miller is unknown in this country because he represents the Continental rather than the English influence. He breaks with the English literary tradition just as many of the twentieth-century Americans do, because his ancestry is not British, and not American colonial. He does not read the favored British writers, Milton, Marlowe, Pope, Donne. He reads what his grandparents knew was in the air when Victorianism was the genius of British poetry. He grew up with books by Dostoyevsky, Knut Hamsun, Strindberg, Nietzsche (especially Nietzsche), Elie Faure, Spengler. Like a true poet he found his way to Rimbaud, Ramakrishna, Blavatsky, Huysmans, Count Keyserling, Prince Kropotkin, Lao-tse, Nostradamus, Petronius, Rabelais, Suzuki, Zen philosophy, Van Gogh. And in English he let himself be influenced not by the solid classics but by *Alice in Wonderland*, Chesterton's St. Francis, Conrad, Cooper, Emerson, Rider Haggard, G. A. Henty (the boy's historian—I remember being told when I was a boy that Henty had the facts all wrong), Joyce, Arthur Machen, Mencken, John Cowper Powys, Herbert Spencer's *Autobiography*, Thoreau on "Civil Disobedience," Emma Goldman—the great anarchist (whom he met)—Whitman, of course, and perhaps above all that companion piece to *Leaves of Grass* called *Huckleberry Finn*. Hardly a Great Books list from the shores of Lake Michigan—almost a period list. Miller will introduce his readers to strange masterpieces like Doughty's *Arabia Deserta* or to the journal of Anaïs Nin which has never been published but which he (and other writers) swears is one of the masterpieces of the twentieth century. I imagine that Miller has read as much as any man living but he does not have that religious solemnity about books which we are brought up in. Books,

after all, are only mnemonic devices; and poets are always celebrating the burning of libraries. And as with libraries, so with
monuments, and as with monuments, so with civilizations. But in
Miller's case (chez Miller) there is no vindictiveness, no bitter-
ness. Orwell was bothered when he met Miller because Miller
didn't want to go to the Spanish Civil War and do battle on one
side or the other. Miller is an anarchist of sorts, and he doesn't
especially care which dog eats which dog. As it happens, the
righteous Loyalists were eaten by the Communists and the
righteous Falangists were eaten by the Nazis over the most decadent hole in Europe; so Miller was right.

Lawrence Durrell has said that the *Tropic* books were healthy
while Céline and D. H. Lawrence were sick. Lawrence never
escaped his puritanism and it is his heroic try that makes us
honor him. Céline is the typical European man of despair—why
should he not despair, this Frenchman of the trenches of World
War I? We are raising up a generation of young American Célines,
I'm afraid, but Miller's generation still had Whitman before its
eyes and was not running back to the potholes and ash heaps of
Europe. Miller is as good an antiquarian as anybody; in the
medieval towns of France he goes wild with happiness; and he has
written one of the best "travel books" on Greece ever done (the
critics are unanimous about the *Colossus of Maroussi*); but to
worship the "tradition" is to him the sheerest absurdity. Like
most Americans, he shares the view of the first Henry Ford that
history is bunk. He cannot forgive his "Nordic" ancestors for the
doctrines of righteousness and cleanliness. His people, he says,
were painfully clean: "Never once had they opened the door
which leads to the soul; never once did they dream of taking a
blind leap into the dark. After dinner the dishes were promptly
washed and put in the closet; after the paper was read it was
neatly folded and laid away on a shelf; after the clothes were
washed they were ironed and folded and then tucked away in the
drawers. Everything was for tomorrow, but tomorrow never came.
The present was only a bridge and on this bridge they are still
groaning, as the world groans, and not one idiot ever thinks of
blowing up the bridge." As everyone knows, cleanliness is the
chief American industry. Miller is the most formidable anticlean-

liness poet since Walt Whitman, and his hatred of righteousness
is also American, with the Americanism of Thoreau, Whitman,
and Emma Goldman. Miller writes a good deal about cooking
and wine drinking. Americans are the worst cooks in the world,
outside of the British; and Americans are also great drunkards
who know nothing about wine. The Germanic-American Miller
reintroduces good food and decent wine into our literature. One
of his funniest essays is about the American loaf of bread, the
poisonous loaf of cleanliness wrapped in cellophane, the manu-
facture of which is a heavy industry like steel.

Orwell and other critics tend to regard Miller as a kind of
hedonist and professional do-nothing. And morally, they tend to
regard him as one of that illustrious line of Americans who
undermine the foundations of traditional morals. Miller quotes
Thoreau's statement, which might almost be the motto of the
cosmic writer: "Most of what my neighbors call good, I am profoundly convinced is evil, and if I repent anything, it is my good
conduct that I repent." One could hardly call Thoreau a criminal,
yet he had his run ins with the law, just as Miller has, and for
the same reasons. The strain of anarchism and amorality is growing stronger in American literature, or that branch of it that I am
talking about, and Miller is one of its chief carriers. It is not only
Emma Goldman, Thoreau, Mark Twain, Whitman, and perhaps
Salinger, but that whole literature of Detachment from political
hysteria and overorganization. I am influenced enough by these
people and by Miller to tell my students, the poets at least, to
cultivate an ignorance of contemporary political and military
events because they do not matter. I tell them not to vote, to join
nothing. I try to steer them toward their true leaders and visionaries, men almost unknown in the polite literary world, Reich for
instance. Wilhelm Reich furthered a movement in Germany called
"Work Democracy"; not machine politics, no politics at all, but
democracy within one's immediate orbit; democracy at home.
America is still the only country where social idealism and experi-
mentation have elbow room; there are still communities that practice primitive Christianity, such as the Catholic anarchists; and
just plain little homemade gardens of Eden such as Miller's cliff

at Big Sur. The life he describes in *Big Sur and the Oranges of Hieronymus Bosch* is a far cry from the little fascist dreams of the New Classicists. And it is a far cry from the bitter isolationism of Robinson Jeffers or even of Lawrence. Morally I regard Miller as a holy man, as most of his adherents do—Gandhi with a penis.

Miller says in a little essay on Immorality and Morality: "What is moral and what is immoral? Nobody can ever answer this question satisfactorily. Not because morals ceaselessly evolve, but because the principle on which they depend is fictitious. Morality is for slaves, for beings without spirit. And when I say spirit I mean the Holy Spirit." And he ends this little piece with a quotation from ancient Hindu scripture: "Evil does not exist."

Whitman, Lawrence, Miller, and even Blake all have the reputation of being sex-obsessed, Miller especially. Whereas Whitman writes "copulation is no more rank to me than death is," Miller writes hundreds of pages describing in the minutest and clearest detail his exploits in bed. Every serious reader of erotica has remarked about Miller that he is probably the only author in history who writes about such things with complete ease and naturalness. Lawrence never quite rid himself of his puritanical salaciousness, nor Joyce; both had too much religion in their veins. It is funny to recollect that Lawrence thought *Ulysses* a smutty book and Joyce thought *Lady Chatterley* a smutty book. Both were right. But at least they *tried* to free themselves from literary morality. Miller's achievement is miraculous: he is screamingly funny without making fun of sex, the way Rabelais does. (Rabelais is, of course, magnificent; so is Boccaccio; but both write against the background of religion, like Joyce and Lawrence.) Miller is accurate and poetic in the highest degree; there is not a smirk anywhere in his writings. Miller undoubtedly profited from the mistakes of his predecessors; his aim was not to write about the erotic but to write the whole truth about the life he knew. This goal demanded the full vocabulary and iconography of sex, and it is possible that he is the first writer outside the Orient who has succeeded in writing as naturally about sex on a large scale as novelists ordinarily write about the dinner table or the battlefield. I think only an American could have performed this feat.

Miller has furthered literature for all writers by ignoring the art forms, the novel, the poem, the drama, and by sticking to the autobiographical novel. He says in *The Books in My Life* (one of the available works), "The autobiographical novel, which Emerson predicted would grow in importance with time, has replaced the great confessions. It is not a mixture of truth and fiction, this genre of literature, but an expansion and deepening of truth. It is more authentic, more veridical, than the diary. It is not the flimsy truth of facts which the authors of these autobiographical novels offer but the truth of emotion, reflection and understanding, truth digested and assimilated. The being revealing himself does so on all levels simultaneously." Everything Miller has written is part of this great amorphous autobiographical novel and it must be read not entirely but in large chunks to make sense. Many of the individual works are whole in themselves, one dealing with his life in Paris, one with his life as a New Yorker, and there is, in fact, a definite span of years encompassed in the works. But the volumes of essays are also part of the story and there is no way to make a whole out of the parts. Miller is easy to quote if one quotes carefully; the danger is that one can find massive contradictions, unless there is some awareness of the underlying world and the cosmic attitudes of the author. These views are by no means unique, as they are the same as those of all those poets and mystics I referred to in a previous essay. What makes Miller unique is his time and place; he is the only American of our time who has given us a full-scale interpretation of modern America, other than the kind of thing we find in the cultural journals. Incidentally, we do not find Miller in these journals, which, presuming an interest in letters and art, are really organs of social and political opinion.

Readers of Whitman recall that Whitman was blistering about the materialism of this country a century ago, and its departure from the ideals of the founding fathers. Miller is worse. Now it is a commonplace of modern poetry that the poet dissociates himself from life as it is lived by the average American today.

Whitman and Miller heap abuse on the failure of the country to live up to its promise. Miller writes as a poet about the demonic hideousness of New York City, Chicago, the South, or he rhapsodizes when there is anything to be rapturous about. But it is not Art that he cares about; it is man, man's treatment of man in America and man's treatment of nature. What we get in Miller is not a sense of superiority but fury, even the fury of the prophet of doom.

Combating the "system" is nonsense. There is only one aim in life and that is to live it. In America it has become impossible, except for a few lucky or wise people, to live one's own life; consequently the poets and artists tend to move to the fringes of society. Wherever there are individuals, says Miller (like Thoreau) there are new frontiers. The American way of life has become illusory; we lead the lives of prisoners while we boast about free speech, free press, and free religion, none of which we actually do enjoy in full. The price for security has become too great; abundance has become a travesty. The only thing for nonenslaved man to do is to move to the edge, lose contact with the machines of organization which are ubiquitous in this country as in Russia. "Instead of bucking your head against a stone wall, sit quietly with hands folded and wait for the walls to crumble. . . . Don't sit and *pray* that it will happen! Just sit and *watch* it happen!" These sayings the culture litterateur condemns as irresponsible. Miller follows through with the complete program of nonparticipation in our machine society, which is organized from the cradle to the grave. "Just as Gandhi successfully exploited the doctrine of nonresistance, so these 'saints of the just' practiced non-recognition—non-recognition of sin, guilt, fear and disease . . . even death." Whitman also believed in non-recognition of death. His view of death as part of life is one of the many reasons for his unpopularity in America, where death is considered a crime against society. "Why try to solve a problem? *Dissolve* it! [says Miller]. Fear not to be a coward, a traitor, a renegade. In this universe of ours there is room for all, perhaps even need for all. The sun does not inquire about rank and status before shedding its warmth; the cyclone levels the godly and the ungodly; the government takes your tax money even though it be tainted. Nor is the atom bomb a respecter of persons. Perhaps that is why the righteous are squirming so!"

Miller calls for an end to revolt once and for all. His message is precisely that of Whitman, of Rimbaud, of Rilke: "Everything we are taught is false"; and "Change your life." As a writer Miller may be second- or third-rate or of no rating at all; as a spiritual example he stands among the great men of our age. Will this ever be recognized? Not in our time probably.

HENRY MILLER AND JOHN BETJEMAN:
PUZZLES AND EPIPHANIES

Frank Kermode

It is often said that Miller and criticism are mutually repel-
lent, and this view accounts for the way critics have left him alone,
an extraordinary neglect considering his reputation and readership
and the endless flow of sophisticated comment on modern, and
especially American, literature. The main exception is George
Orwell's famous essay *Inside the Whale*—but Orwell specialized
in criticizing what others wouldn't touch. Of more recent studies
I know only two of merit, by Philip Rahv and Alwyn Lee. Mr.
Rahv says that the highbrow critics snub Miller because "he
makes bad copy for them," and that the author's admirers are bad
witnesses because of their cultist attachment. The trouble with
the critics is rather, I think, that they see no way of getting a
firm grip on Miller without seeming to identify themselves with
his view of literature. But if criticism is worth anything, as they
presumably believe, even if he does not, they ought to feel
obliged to try; whether or not he is listening is unimportant.
The whole question is whether Miller has any significance outside
the cult, and it is for the critics to say, regardless of the reaction.
The position is, in a different degree, like that of a man writing
about Durrell: if he says he likes some of it, or even all of it with
reservations, the cultists react with insults: provincial! puritan!
critic!

The critic has, in fact, two answers to the devotees. The first is spirited but not very useful; he can borrow Miller's admirable vocabulary of abuse (which is roughly the same as his sexual vocabulary) and apply it to the worst of the sage's writing. Secondly, he can show that the anti-critical attitude of Miller is only an aspect of his profound but very conventional distrust of literature. *"I am not interested in literature,"* he says in his *Open Letter to Surrealists Everywhere;* and in *Capricorn* he discourses quite in the mediaeval manner, on the two kinds of book: one the sort men write, the other made up of "things like toe-nails, hair, blood, *ovaries,* if you will"—the book of life; and this is his option. When he turns critic it is either to write rave notices for his friends or, in a tone of considerable critical solemnity, to explain artists who treat art as "a substitute for life"—Joyce in whom he observes "a dervish dance on the periphery of meaning, an orgasm not of blood and semen but of dead slag," and Proust, "in his classic retreat from life the very symbol of the modern artist." These views are expressed with clarity and force, but in the last analysis are designed for "the maudlin boosting of the ego" (Philip Rahv's phrase) only less directly than usual; they amount to criticism turned against literature, the suborning of a servant. What never seems to have occurred to Miller is that this disgust with *littérature* is very literary, a tired posture at best; and part of the central muddle in this writer is that he makes his nihilistic gestures from a pulpit of very commonplace design. He entirely underestimates the penetrative power of literary tradition, and imagines himself an inspired autodidact, when he is merely an uncritical and random student. The critic can at least say what is commonplace in Miller's anti-literature.

Orwell did this, and called Miller a belated member of the lost generation, a Bohemian lapsed into total proletarianism—not in the garrets of Mürger's Paris but in the streets Orwell knew well, "the cobbled alleys, the sour reek of refuse, the bistros with their greasy zinc counters," etc. Miller, to start with, lives a literary myth, and he neglects no aspect of it in his books. He is a literary person, offering no special stumbling-block to routine critical procedures. The *vie de Bohème* is set in a corrupt metropolis with a literary equivalent that might be called *l'immonde cité.*

The population of Paris, the Paris of the myth, has not changed between Baudelaire and Miller: *L'hôpital se remplit de leurs soupirs.* Here, then, is the artist in his corrupt city, the man of free spirit defying a "Faustian culture." The city is not only Paris, which Miller liked because the mud was deeper and the dives more numerous, but the whole U. S. A. and the other "puritan cultures" of the North. There are vast tracts of lively writing about this and occasionally they are magnificent—for example, the attacks on American bread in *Remember to Remember,* which starts from the loaf and passes on to account for everything that has gone wrong and why in the history of civilization, describes a scene of wild comic frustration in a restaurant, and ends like this:

> Accept any loaf that is offered you without question even if it is not wrapped in cellophane, even if it contains no kelp. Throw it in the back of the car with the oil can and the grease rags; if possible, bury it under a sack of coal, *bituminous* coal. As you climb up the road to your home, drop it in the mud a few times and dig your heels into it. When you get to the house, and after you have prepared the other dishes, take a huge carving knife and rip the loaf from stem to stern. Then take one whole onion, peeled or unpeeled, one carrot, one stalk of celery, one huge piece of garlic, one sliced apple, a herring, a handful of anchovies, a sprig of parsley, and an old toothbrush, and shove them in the disembowelled guts of the bread. Over these pour a thimbleful of kerosene, a dash of Lavoris, and just a wee bit of Clorox. . . .

and so on. All this is Miller kicking around the American way of life—"cancer, syphilis, arthritis, tuberculosis, schizophrenia are so prevalent that we accept them as part of the bargain—i.e., the American way of life"—*l'immonde cité* corrupts even the staff of life. Of course he manages to be gay or boisterous about it; that is part of the artist's bargain; and he adds to an absurd savagery of expression a capacity for falling in love with the hated object, as in the brilliant automobile passage in *The Air-Conditioned Nightmare*. But the basic situation is: artist in slum civilization. And very much *in* it; the hero of *Capricorn*, seen from the outside, is only a madder version of Mr. Eliot's carbuncular clerk.

The obscenity which keeps so much of Miller under the counter is an element of this city-myth. He himself defends it like an old literary hand.

> I am in the tradition . . . a list of my precursors would make an impressive roster. . . . In the not too distant past there was one who was given the cup of hemlock for being "the corrupter of youth." To-day he is regarded as one of the sanest, most lucid minds that ever was.

(Or, as Miller put it, "Mankind can hardly be too often reminded, that there was once a man named Socrates, between whom and the legal authorities and public opinion of his time, there took place a memorable collision.") "How," Miller continues, "can one guard against evil . . . if one does not know what evil is?" (Or, as Milton might have said, the obscenities are there "that we may see and know, and yet abstain.") Perfectly orthodox; obscenity is merely a matter of technique, of establishing the need of the artist to escape from *l'immonde cité*. *The Tropic of Cancer,* says Miller, is concerned

> not with sex, nor with religion, but with the problem of self-liberation . . . a blood-soaked testament revealing the ravages of my struggle in the womb of death.

You can almost hear the expert witnesses talking about Miller as if he were Baudelaire, or invoking the "puritan tradition." But these words of his seem only very loosely applicable to his texts, which do not seem to me to make it clear that random copulation is a *terminus a quo* rather than *ad quem*. He dwells on the details of love-making with dwarfs or mental defectives, or handy car pickups, on the sheer fun of having Rita in the vestibule. People do, of course, live like the hero of the *Tropics*, but he is given a legendary Paul Bunyan-like potency, and sometimes the point made by a sexual adventure is precisely that of the *fabliau* (there is an example in *Capricorn* of extreme antiquity), or the tall story, or the Rabelaisian fantasy—his meditations while in conjunction with the mental defective have the true Rabelaisian range of vocabulary and learning. But what has all this "lucubration," as he calls it, to do with rebirth, the escape from a debased sexuality? It is the work of a *voyou* with logorrhea. The one thing Miller has in common with Lawrence is his high valuation of sex as an indication of cultural dilapidation, and of primitive sexuality as a criterion; but they could hardly be more different in their application of these beliefs, which take Miller into Juanist fantasy and, weirdly, into comedy; the farcical vision of love in the world's infancy (*Capricorn*) is, though unquotable, probably the finest passage he ever wrote. Lawrence would probably have called it obscene, an urban dirty joke.

Miller's relations with *l'immonde cité* are, then, ambiguous, but what he says they are is clear enough, and perfectly orthodox. He often writes about the artist in society, and what he says bears out this statement. The artist, or even the man who produces nothing but *lives* like an artist, may claim special privileges: the ultimate defence of Bohemianism.

> The life of the artist is the highest and the last phase of egotism in man. . . . The goal is liberation, freedom, . . . to continue writing beyond the point of self-realization seems futile and arresting . . . one is absolutely alone.

But this is a costly privilege and costly achievement.

No man *wants* to be an artist—he is driven to it.

The agony of a Christ on Calvary illustrates superbly the ordeal which even a Master must undergo in the creation of a perfect life.

Now this image of the artist "crucified and marked by the cross" has a venerable place in Romantic iconography, and goes back through Lawrence and Yeats and Wilde to Kierkegaard. And it will come as no surprise that Miller worships Rimbaud. It is the ritual-torture element in the big nineteenth-century myth that fascinates him; his variation is a simple conversion of guilt into defiance. Instead of the old vision of the gibbet and the old cry:

> *Ah! Seigneur! donnez-moi la force et le courage*
> *De contempûler mon coeur et mon corps sans dégout!*

he offers the guttersnipe ecstasies of *Capricorn,* copulation performed as an act of vengeance: "somebody had to pay for making me walk around in the rain grubbing for a dime. Somebody had to pay for the ecstasy produced by the germination of all those unwritten books inside me." The visionary artist modulates into the shouting figure in search of ecstasy or a girl, with *Creative Evolution* under his arm, composing his own *historia calamitatum* and ignoring everybody else's; living inside the whale.

Orwell's admiration for this characteristic of Miller's was in part a reaction from what he regarded as the pert and immature political opinions of the 'thirties poets, and he over-estimated what he called the American's power of not being frightened. But he was much too shrewd not to notice that the force which kept Miller out of politics was a very literary primitivism; he saw that all the "change-of-heart" men were fundamentally pessimistic because what they have is

a wish that things would happen in a way which they are manifestly not going to happen. . . . Our eyes are directed

> to Rome, to Byzantium, to Montparnasse, to Mexico, to
> the Etruscans, to the Subconscious, to the solar plexus—to
> everywhere except the places where things are actually
> happening.

And although he sees some good in this so far as Miller is concerned, he correctly associates these views with prevailing literary
fashion which the 'thirties merely interrupted for a while. I don't
know of any better way to "place" Miller for outsiders than to
catalogue briefly some of the ways in which he is in thrall to the
conventions of modern Romantic primitivism, wherever he may
have encountered them; characteristically he thinks his views may
have welled up from "the universal memory." I have already mentioned the hatred of *littérature,* so I don't include that, or the
related fondness for illiterates, which he shares with otherwise
diverse figures as Yeats, Eliot, Valéry, Lawrence, and Wallace
Stevens.

First, and this is the radical one, is Miller's *anti-intellectualism.* The position is stated with extreme naïveté in the story
Picodiribibi, reprinted by Mr. Durrell.

> When man ate of the Tree of Knowledge he elected
> to find a short-cut to godhood. He attempted to rob the
> Creator of the divine secret, which to him spelled power.
> What has been the result? Sin, disease, death. Eternal war-
> fare, eternal unrest. The little we know we use for our
> own destruction.

Consequently he has an extreme but conventional contempt for
scientific thought, for all kinds of abstraction; and a respect for
"things." In *Capricorn* the *logos* is described as the root of evil,
and rejected in favour of the "worthless *thing*" that contains "the
secret of my own regeneration." "'If you can't give the is-ness of
a thing, give the not-ness of it," he advises; and appears (igno-
rantly, in my view) to praise Swift for doing so. There is no need

to dwell upon the antecedents and analogues of this attitude. From it there flows naturally two consequential doctrines: a straightforward chronological primitivism, and a fashionable occultism.

As to the first of these, "savages" have a "greater hold on reality" than we; they are more intelligent, too. Miller's own intelligence is "savage." There was a time when everybody was savage, and the world had a fiercely-coloured priapic beauty. But there has been a catastrophe, a dissociation of man from the world, reflected in "the loss of sex polarity." When did this occur? "The great Shakespearean dramas were but the announcement" of it. We have certainly been here, or hereabouts, before.

Why do people who think along these lines almost always take up with the occult? Because it has been since the Romantic movement (what it was for a time in the seventeenth century) the seductively obvious alternative to Science. It is an inexhaustible study, full of fascinating analogies and sudden confirmations, and very congenial to the generally syncretic cast of the literary mind; there is no end to its platonic, cabbalist, hermetic, theosophical, and Buddhist ramifications. Among the small group of Americans Miller admires is a learned Freemason, who says:

> religions decay into idle forms and the mummery of meaningless words. The Symbols remain, like the sea shells washed up from the depths, motionless and dead. . . . Shall it always be so with Masonry, likewise? Or shall its ancient Symbols, inherited by it from the primitive faiths and most ancient initiations, be rescued from the enthralment of commonplace and trivial misinterpretation, be restored to their ancient high estate and again become the Holy Oracles of philosophical and religious Truth, their revelation of Divine Wisdom to our thoughtful ancestors?

Miller marvels that in an age given over to "crass materialism" there should survive so great a scholar, sage, Cabbalist, Hermetist, etc. By the same token his favorite nineteenth-century French thinker is Eliphas Lévi, and he hardly needs to add that he also admires Balzac—the Balzac of *Louis Lambert* and *Seraphita*. Among the photographs on his wall are those of Khrishnamurti and Rimbaud. (He is remarkably like Yeats in these matters, though less learned and less discriminating.) Another hero is Rider Haggard.

The link between modern art and occultism is strong and obvious; Symons made it plain in the dedication of *The Symbolist Movement*. Art works like "magic" or "mysticism"—terms that are not clearly distinguished. Like them it is independent of intellect and deals in a superior kind of reality, where spirit and sense are not dissociated. Like magic, art depends upon symbols, and upon the common stock of symbol and myth, to which it achieves a non-intellective access. "I prefer music above all the arts. . . . I believe that literature, to become truly communicable . . . must make greater use of the symbol and the metaphor, of the mythological and the archaic." (How's that for commonplace?) Art must be freshened up like the Masonic Symbols.

The reward of the artist who works in this way is precisely that of the mystic; he penetrates the flux, achieves union with reality. Miller often tells us what this feels like, but his terms are not unfamiliar in other artists. "Walking back and forth over Brooklyn Bridge everything became crystal clear to me." It is not necessarily a pleasant experience; there may come "a sense of desolation truly unprecedented. . . . 'I' was absent. . . ." But sometimes it is: "I was standing in my own presence bathed in a luminous reality." Sometimes Miller talks like a Baroque saint of "the miraculous wound which I received, the wound which killed me in the eyes of the world and out of which I was born anew."

This is again an aspect of a familiar myth, but it is unusually important to Miller, and the book which says most about this kind of experience is, in my view, also his best: *The Colossus of Maroussi*. The expression of the mystical experience is in this book sometimes so old-fashioned that it reminds one of *The Prelude*. "Certain spots stand out like semaphores . . . provided . . . they are approached with utter purity of heart"—topographical locations, not spots of time as in Wordsworth, because Miller found in Greece a place he could associate with his special mystical experience. It is what one would expect of his sensitivity to well-established currents of thought that Miller's Greece is not the early-Romantic Greece of Shelley or of Byron but a later, post-Jane Harrison and also post-Otto version. In it he can feel most strongly the lost power of "seeing past and future as one." (His respect for scholarship is shown in a list of the "courageous pioneers" who helped to "break the spell of defeat and paralysis" imposed by nineteenth-century rationalism: Schliemann, Sir Arthur Evans, Frazer, Frobenius, Annie Besant, Madame Blavatsky, Paul Radin, carrying on the work of Henty, Bulwer-Lytton, Marie Corelli, and Rider Haggard.) In the passages on Eleusis, Poros, and Epidaururs, Miller certainly achieves a kind of magnificence, and a familiar sense of regeneration:

> This is the first day of my life . . . that I have included everybody and everything on this earth in one thought. . . . I bless the world, every inch of it, every living atom, and it is all alive.

Even at his finest and most individual Miller reminds us of finer artists, artists who do not despise *mesure*.

I do not suggest that this survey of the conventional elements in Miller has any very direct bearing upon his quality as a writer, or as a sage. It is merely a matter of saying, for outsiders, what sort of a writer he is. The question of his merit is the one that his admirers will never allow a critic to settle. It will, however, be agreed on both sides that his gift depends on the power to depose intellect, to frighten away *mesure;* hence his uneasy relation with surrealism and the respect with which he quotes Dadaist spells. The price he pays, in the words of Alwyn Lee, is that he abondons the power to distinguish between art and piffle, in others as well as in himself. Everybody agrees that Miller *can* write; his is a curious gift, incapable of any kind of rest, dependent on continuous movement. The torrent, brilliant or piffling, rolls on; at its best it has the surge and glitter of—Crashaw, a name that suits the Baroque cast of his spirituality: blood pours, eyes roll, the angel plunges his weapon into the saint, whose draperies defy the law of gravity. Miller throws himself on the language, as upon books and people. He is as he describes Katsimbalis in the *Colossus,*

> alive and flourishing like a smoking dung-heap. He could galvanize the dead with his talk. It was a sort of devouring process, when he described a place he ate into it, like a goat attacking a carpet. If he described a person he ate him alive from head to toe.

What, as one rolls down the stream, tells one whether this time it is art or piffle? It is the question that Miller claims to be unanswerable; he wants only surrender to the current. Joyce made great demands too, but the qualities that make us respect him as an artist are the same that made Miller speak of him as in love with death. Life, and therefore Miller, deny "form" and *mesure.* So the critic labels him a minor figure and stands by for perfectly predictable insults.

The Sixties

The sixties was a decade of reassessment of Henry Miller. David Littlejohn's review is a remarkably concise enumeration of those aspects of Miller's work which proved to be the critical areas that required revaluation. Of the literally thousands of book reviews of one or another of Miller's works, Littlejohn's is one of the few that attains to the level of criticism. It commences with an announcement of the subject's chief value as the reviewer sees it. It places the author in a literary tradition and calls attention to the strengths and weaknesses of the author's use of that tradition—in Miller's case the at best "as if" sense of conviction that his prophetic, apocalyptic posture is capable of stirring in the reader. Finally, it cites specifically the weaknesses which are most likely to detract from the reader's empathetic involvement in Miller's world.

Like Alwyn Lee, Littlejohn considers Miller's "total detachment" to be his most distinguishing characteristic. But, while he agrees that such detachment has its price, he concludes that the cost is personal, in that he lost potential readers, rather than symptomatic of pathological malaise. Furthermore the advantages —a devastating quality of honesty, a virtually "pre-civilized" point

97

of view, and a moving romantic idealism—outweigh the disadvantages because it is the "projected personality" of Henry Miller which is the enlarging experience for the reader.

Kingsley Widmer's book for the Twayne United States Authors Series is the first full-length study of Henry Miller from a critical, as distinct from a biographical or reminiscent, point of view. Widmer's most noteworthy achievement may be that he manages to steer an admirable course between what have proven to be the Scylla and Charybdis of the criticism of Miller. He neither indulges in a hasty celebration of Miller as a torchbearer of the Romantic tradition, nor does he dismiss Miller as one who essayed such a role but failed. As Widmer sees it, Miller is a Rebel-Buffoon, and the hyphen in that title is as important as both of the nouns.

Widmer calls Miller's main creation the "rhetoric of grotesquerie." His influence, which may have been more pervasive than previously recognized, has issued mainly from that rhetoric, particularly as it has evolved in the work of poets like Ferlinghetti, Corso and Ginsberg. But such rhetoric, "surreal, obscene, fantastic, iconoclastic, learned, colloquial, lavish and desperate" is inescapably buffoonish. Indeed, the buffoon inflates himself, reels into the ludicrous, in order that we may see things in perspective. Yet, Widmer maintains, such buffoonery is an important rebellion, particularly when adventure into a closed, personal world and rebellion against an amorphous doom are both equally foolish. "But the Millerian grotesque makes the rhetorical gestures of adventure, and he rebels by refusing heroic poses as well as victimization. Thus to insist on one's grotesqueness is to insist on one's being—a residual, inverted, yet finally crucial heroism."

Widmer's is a valuable effort to trace Miller's path in a universe of literary history crowded with bodies varying in luminosity but tracing more erratic orbits than is perhaps generally acknowledged. Not the least of the essay's merits is the reminder that "while Miller is minor writer, he may—in his best work—have a major relevance."

Sidney Finkelstein's approach to Miller is important for two reasons. First, his criticisms issue from a firmly held view of the relationship between a society and the process of history. Second, he is one of the few critics who devotes explicit attention to Miller's relation to existentialism. Finkelstein accounts for the relationship by urging that "what brings Miller to an existentialist position is his search for some human basis for living, which he can assert in the face of a world he regards as inimical and absurd." As I have suggested in my introduction, it may be open to question whether it is "the world" which Miller finds inimical and absurd, but there is no question that his alienation issues from a search for a new basis from which to live humanly.

The relationship between a society and its artists, and more generally, society and history might with justice be called the essential issue underlying virtually all of the commentary on Henry Miller. The advantage of Finkelstein's Marxist orientation is that it renders explicit a position which might be appreciated, though for different reasons, by such diverse observers as Orwell and Alwyn Lee. "The truth is," argues Finkelstein, "that rebellions are made in real life, not in art. They occur when conditions for the mass of people become intolerable, and the institutions under which they live, instead of assisting their progress, stifle it. What art has done is progressively to humanize the world and the relations among people in it; to make men aware of their own potentialities. . . ." If artists *are* artists to the degree that they serve to illustrate their society's potentialities in the process of history, then a renunciation of society leads the artist inevitably to a surrender of his humanity. Whatever one's attitude toward his premises, Finkelstein provides a clear basis for a charge which critics have levied against Miller, with varying force, for two decades.

Alan Friedman's essay is reprinted in its entirety for two reasons. Friedman attends to the use of "obscenity" in Miller's writing, noting Stanley Kauffmann's perceptive observation that Miller's books may have been subject to excessive praise "as a tactical move by those interested in the freedom of letters." In view of the fact that all of Miller's so-called obscene work is now readily available, and with the numerous obscenity trials of the *Tropics* a phenomenon of literary history, it may seem profitless to dwell on the issue. As Friedman points out, however, the matter is still very much alive for the literary critic because

"Miller the cause—a Miller obviously noble, obviously on the side of the angels—tends to become inextricable from Miller the artist, a figure of still questionable stature."

Second, Friedman strikes at the heart of the issue of "Miller the artist" with his conclusion that despite the efforts at structuring and the explicit thematic statements, the *Tropics* are "not about redemption at all, but only about the death of love—and the irrevocable finality and waste of one man's spiritual suicide." What is perhaps most important about Friedman's conclusion is not so much that it runs counter to the numerous claims citing Whitmanian romanticism as Miller's temperamental and literary heritage. Rather, its significance lies in the fact that Friedman views Miller's suicidal effort to deny love as a failure. Paradoxically, Miller's pervasive nihilism, his inability to rise from negation to affirmation, itself becomes evidence of "a pervasive disordering," an attempt at negation which, "doomed to failure," affirms what it attempts to deny.

My own essay is the only one of which I am aware that addresses itself entirely to the issue of an aesthetic, that is a more or less conscious conceptualization of the relationship among artist, art and audience, in Miller's work. As I see it, the central issue is Miller's view of what art is and what it ought to do, for this in turn determines for him the role of both artist and audience. Because of Miller's yoking of the "poet" with the "seer," it might be advantageous to compare my approach with that of Wallace Fowlie who, as I have previously indicated, addresses in part the same issues. The fact that I place Miller in the context of Plato's *Republic* argues that I see Miller's aesthetic in an ideological context very much different from that of Sidney Finkelstein.

The danger in taking my approach is that it gives the impression that Miller is more of a systematic thinker than he in fact is. Perhaps what ought to be said is that few artists *are* aestheticians, in the sense of arguing a system of thought, but all *practice* an aesthetic of some variety, and Miller is no exception. I believe it behooves us to make what efforts we can to understand the artist's view of his role and the nature and function of his art, for our most meaningful relationships with him, both positive and negative, lie at this level.

The selection included here from William Gordon's book on Henry Miller is a fitting close to this collection because it relates in multiple ways to those issues which three decades of criticism have established as central to an informed understanding of Miller and his art. The autobiographical form, the idea of self-creation and its relation to the subconscious as a reservoir of meaning and form, the use of fantasy and the experience of cosmic consciousness —all of these are discussed by Gordon. Mere recapitulation, however, is not Gordon's intention. While he views Miller as firmly rooted in the Romantic tradition, he is explicit in remarking the differences between the earlier romantics and those who found themselves in a world virtually reshaped by Darwin, Freud, and Einstein. The key to Miller's essential seriousness lies, as Gordon sees it, in the autobiographical form—the formal structuring of the search for individual identity—which is the essence of his art. Likening the structure of Romantic autobiographical art to that of the fugue, Gordon observes that "the overall theme is based on the idea of growth toward fulfillment, of the conversion of vital energy into form, which enhances the individual's sense of identity and completion."

It is enlightening to consider earlier insights—those of Hoffman, Fowlie, Widmer, for example—and preceding critical reservations like those of Orwell, Lee, and Kermode, in light of Gordon's effort to view Miller steadily and whole. But perhaps most rewarding of all is the fact that Gordon places Miller within a context of ongoing tradition, the perseverance and vitality of which is once again coming to be appreciated.

THE TROPICS OF MILLER

David Littlejohn

The most lasting, affecting experience of fighting one's way through the tropics of Miller is meeting the man who built them. Everything he has ever written is a piece of ever-in-progress autobiography, a continuing *romanfleuve* of The Life of Henry Miller. He quoted Emerson for the epigraph to *Tropic of Cancer:* "These novels will give way, by and by, to diaries and autobiographies—captivating books, if only a man knew how to choose among what he calls experience that which is really his experience, and how to record truth truly." And he has been trying to live up to the prophecy ever since. *Tropic of Cancer,* first published in 1934, is the story of his days (and nights) in Paris and Dijon in the early 1930's. *Tropic of Capricorn* returns us to the five years he spent working in New York, from 1920 to '24. *Black Spring* records, among other things, his turn-of-the-century boyhood in Brooklyn. *The Colossus of Maroussi* and *The Air-Conditioned Nightmare* are "travel books" of a sort, recollections of trips through Greece and America made near the beginning of the war. *The World of Sex* and *The Rosy Crucifixion* trilogy now in progress take most of their material again from New York in the 1920's, and in *Big Sur and the Oranges of Hieronymous Bosch* Miller tells of his life on the California coast since 1944. The articles and short stories collected in several other books are all equally autobiographical, all pieces in the ever-growing puzzle of the whole.

In an age of pervasive and overwhelming social integration, Miller has achieved the all-but-impossible stance of total detachment. He is an Individualist so extreme as to seem at times prehistoric. He is above or below, or beyond, or apart from all our most intimate social concerns. Clashes of ideology, affairs of state, scientific achievements "progress" in every sense, the whole complex of reservations and deceptions and expectations that makes social living possible—with all of these, Miller is uninvolved.

So total a withdrawal has its cost: Miller has been epically unsuccessful, both denounced and unread for most of his adult life. But if the position of detachment has its misfortunes, it has also its rewards, rewards of no small consequence to the reader of Henry Miller. His lifelong "commitment" has yielded a unique and devastating quality of honesty in almost all of his works. There is no hesitation, no withdrawal, not the slightest touch of reticence; neither does he boast of all his sordid adventures and criminal emotions. They are simply there, for better or worse. This is how it was. No other author has seen fit to record as such ugly matter-of-fact every last crumb of existence. Few admit such things to themselves. For the reader, the experience is likely to be disturbing and totally new.

A second advantage of this unenviable commitment is the faculty of "pre-civilized vision" the artist acquires. He becomes able to *see* with a stunning, primordial strangeness. The effect, once again, is devastating. Most of the scrofulous images in the *Tropics* result from this precivilized vision, this faculty of seeing latent correspondences which shock the civilized sensibility: a face "nothing but a skull perforated by two deep sockets in which there are buried a pair of dead clams." . . . Civilization "rotting like the toenails of the saints," worshippers "like a million heads of cauliflower wailing in the dark," "asses smooth as the skull of a leper." We are shocked (and the shock is every bit intended) partly because we are not used to seeing such things in print—we cannot, that is, share the author's freedom from a civilized sensibility. But also because the author has penetrated to an elemental and singularly effective source of imagery—the deepest-lying levels of consciousness.

A third result of Miller's epic egocentricity is a blessing somewhat more mixed. He is first and always writing for himself; but like his grandfathers Lawrence and Whitman and Blake, he feels compelled time and again to speak out to the abandoned world. Miller the doom-shouting apocalyptic critic, Miller the arch-romantic idealistic prophet can be somewhat less than convincing. At best, his own eloquent and evident conviction can move, stir us "as if" we believed.

"If at intervals of centuries there does appear a man with a desperate, hungry look in his eye, a man who would turn the world upside down in order to create a new race, the love that he brings to the world is turned to bile and he becomes a scourge. If now and then we encounter pages that explode, pages that wound and scar, know that they come from a man with his back up, a man whose only defenses left are his words and his words are always stronger than the lying, crushing weight of the world, stronger than all the racks and wheels which the cowardly invent to crush out the miracle of personality. . . . Let us have more oceans, more upheavals, more wars, more holocausts. Let us have a world of men and women with dynamos between their legs, a world of natural fury, of passion, action, drama, dreams, madness, a world that produces ecstasy. . . ."

This Blakean-Lawrentian ideal, the eternal shout of the earth-man, is as hopelessly unattainable as the Marxist millennium or universal Christian love. It is moving beyond question. But few readers will feel impelled to start smashing the looms or dissolving their civilizations.

What is experienced by the reader in these visions and denunciations (in such few of them, that is, as are vivid and coherent) is, once again, simply "the miracle of personality"— the large and lasting fact of Henry Miller.

When a man like this sets about to write, the result is something altogether strange. There is no shred of a sense of direction either spatial, temporal, or logical to be found in all the chaos of the *Tropics*. Anything ordered, organized, expected, is untrue for Miller: "It is counterfeit," he says. "I felt compelled, in all

honesty, to take the disparate elements of our life . . . and manip-
ulate them through my own personal mode, using my own
shattered and dispersed ego as heartlessly and recklessly as I
would the flotsam and jetsam of the surrounding phenomenal
world. . . ."

There is a felt quality of "writing-in-progress" in Miller's
works, of the author impulsively improvising at the typewriter,
letting a wide-open imagination take him wherever it will. "I have
made a silent compact with myself not to change a line of what I
write. I am not interested in perfecting my thoughts, nor my
action."

Writing oneself out freely and uncritically, as the Surrealists
discovered, may produce only page after page of tedium and in-
coherence. At its liveliest, though, Miller's semi-automatic writing
yields a captivating "musical" quality. Theme merges into theme,
and image into image, exploding at last into wild surrealistic
fantasy.

This same careless directionlessness results in Miller's books
becoming unlikely portmanteaux packed with the oddest acces-
sories. Even *Tropic of Cancer,* which, when it has a plot, is a
picaresque succession of panhandled beds and mindless copulations, finds room for theories of art, a review of Matisse, the end
of the world, Hindu mysticism, Proustian memoirs, and the
thought of Oswald Spengler. In Miller's own terms, such "'digres-
sions" and intrusions are scarcely to be criticized, any more than
the copulations.

Like his character Moldorf, like his friend and champion
Lawrence Durrell—and he can sound *very* like Durrell—Miller
"is word drunk." He delights in characterization by catalogue,
circling round a character or a place with evocative chains of
words or phrases. Like Whitman's endless roll-calls, this can become simply a device for marking time while the mind is disen-
gaged. But here is Tania:

> . . . *les voies urinairs.* Cafe de la Liberte, Place des Vosges,
> bright neckties on the Boulevard Montparnasse, dark bath-

rooms, Porto Sec, Abdullah cigarettes, the adagio sonata pathetique, aural amplificators, anecdotal seances, burnt sienna breasts, heavy garters, what time is it, golden pheasants stuffed with chestnuts, taffeta fingers, vaporish twilights turning to ilex, acromegaly, cancer and delirium, warm veils, poker chips, carpets of blood and soft things.

Like Durrell, too, are the telegraphic scene-setting paragraphs— "Twilight hour, Indian blue, water of glass, trees glistening and liquescent. The rains fall away into the canal at Jaures"— and the fascination with exotic colors. "Vermillion, saffron, mauve, sienna, apricot, turquoise, onyx, Anjou, herring, Corona, verdigris, gorgonzola." . . . "The sun is setting fast. The colors die, they shift from purple to dried blood, from nacre to bistre. . . ." Lines like these could almost serve as parodies of *Justine*, 22 years in advance.

Humor is another quite unexpected reward. Miller alternates in his narrative sequences between droll exaggeration and satire and the wildest of high-humored gusto. The whole chapter on the visiting Indians in *Cancer* is a priceless example of the first; the weekend at Le Havre at the end of the book is perhaps the best of the second. The brilliantly bitter "Via Dieppe-Newhaven" in *The Cosmological Eye*, the outrageous Telegraph Company office fantasy in *Tropic of Capricorn*, his life as a school teacher in Dijon in *Cancer* are masterpieces of comic art. Miller lists in his "genealogical line," along with Lawrence and the Surrealists, the likes of Rabelais, Boccaccio, and Petronius; and the presumption is justified. The best of Miller's pornography, like the best of theirs, is blessed with ludicrous exaggeration.

It is interesting to note that all of these sequences comprise extended, almost uninterrupted sections of straight narration. The Dijon episode takes up 20 pages, the longest unbroken piece of narration in *Tropic of Cancer*. The Telegraph Comany occupies the greater part of the first 50 pages of *Tropic of Capricorn*. This is not, as we have defined it, Miller's natural mode. This is the way of the novelist. What is more, although none of Miller's "reminiscences" escapes exaggeration and distortion—"Every word I say is a lie"—these are clearly the most invented, least autobiographical passages.

In a word, Miller is perhaps most successful, surely most readable, when he adopts the method of the craftsmen of fiction. The most memorable of his characters, too, whatever biographical antecedents they may have had, were certainly born again in Miller's creative imagination. Obscene, unhappy Van Norden, for example, the real Colossus of *Cancer,* is surely too rich and fantastic to have happened anywhere else.

But conscious craft is not the whole art. There is also that "creative imagination," at once the faculty that sees and the faculty that invents. These surrealistic visions may well be the ultimate reach of Miller's accomplishment. The best of them combine the startling immediacy of the "Miller eye," his unique free way of seeing, with the rich rhythms and diction and organization of his art. The best of them, unfortunately, are better left unquoted. But they are like this:

> The earth is not an arid plateau of health and comfort, but a great sprawling female with velvet torso that swells and heaves with ocean billows; she squirms beneath a diadem of sweat and anguish. Naked and sexed she rolls among the clouds in the violet light of the stars. All of her, from her generous breasts to her gleaming thighs, blazes with furious ardor. She moves among the seasons and the years with a grand whoop-la that seizes the torso with paroxysmic fury, that shakes the cobwebs out of the sky.

Which leaves only three things to consider, the three things that are still likely to put most people off from considering Miller at all: the Miller world, the question of pornography, and the tedium.

The Miller world is a rather repulsive place. People with bits of food sticking to their lips are always swabbing themselves for veneral disease in flats smelling of rancid butter. Even exempting the sexual *malaise,* this becomes a little harder to take. The imagery, as we have seen, partakes of the same fetid odor of disease, particularly (as witness the title) in *Tropic of Cancer.* Even spring—"There was a touch of Spring in the air, a poisonous, malefic Spring that seemed to burst from the manholes." Of course. It is so pervasive an atmosphere that, once we learn to breathe, sudden intrusions of the "other" world—*our* world— have the shocking quality of an unexpected grotesque. "A letter arrived from America. Moe is getting A's in everything. Murray is learning to ride the bicycle. The victrola was repaired."

The source of all this, and its justification in Miller's terms, is easy to seek. It derives in part from his unashamed, open-eyed recording of precisely what was: this may well have *been* what was for Miller. It comes, in second part, from the pre-civilized, subconscious correspondences he is particularly apt to discover—at some cost to conscious, post-civilized sensibilities. And finally, as part of his apocalyptic scheme of regeneration, he has, quite frankly, every *intention* of shocking us out of our Puritanic skins. "A man who is intent on creation always dives beneath, to open the wound, to the festering obscene horror. . . . When a hungry, desperate spirit appears and makes the guinea pigs squeal it is because he knows where to put the live wire of sex, because he knows that beneath the hard carapace of indifference there is concealed the ugly gash, the wound that never heals."

These same sources help to explain the unparalleled content of obscenity in Miller's work. "From the point of view of both its happenings and the language in which they are conveyed," Edmund Wilson wrote of *Tropic of Cancer* in 1938, "it is the lowest book of any real literary merit that I ever remember to have read." He might only have wished to revise that judgment the following year, when *Tropic of Capricorn* appeared.

Miller seems to have three approaches to his pornography: the factual, the humorous or hyperbolic, and the truly salacious. The first, which is all too common, is also deadly dull. Matter-of-fact recordings of who, how, and how many times are likely to arouse few erotic impulses. The second escapes the same indictment by taking the opposite extreme. Some of the most agreeable fantasies in the *Tropics* take off from the rankest obscenities;

they explode quickly into cosmic exaggeration far out of reach
of the lecher. The third, I suppose, must remain a matter of taste.
In this respect, the almost mystical sexual experiences of D. H.
Lawrence are often far more affecting, simply because they *are*
idealized. Honest Henry Miller is always hearing springs squeak
or belching or wondering how he can get his money back, and
shattering the dream.

As for "those words," it is perhaps simply a question of ac-
customing oneself, or not. In an amusing passage from a story
called "Astrological Fricassee" (in *Remember to Remember),* set
at a Hollywood party, Miller gives us fair warning not to take
them too seriously:

"What is *your* game?" she asked suddenly.

"My *game?* Oh, I write."

"Go on . . . do you mean it? What sort of stuff? History,
biology . . . ?"

"Naughty books," I said, trying to blush deeply.

"What kind of naughty books? Naughty-naughty—or
just dirt?"

"Just dirt, I guess."

"You mean—Lady Chatterby, or Chattersley, or whatever the hell it is? Not that swill you don't mean, do you?"

I laughed. "No, not that sort . . . just straight obscenity. You know—duck, chit, kiss, trick, punt. . . ."

Still, perhaps Oscar Wilde was right: the only sin is to bore. At
least for a writer.

That a book is nearly impossible to read through need not
rob it of critical esteem. *Finnegans Wake, Remembrance of
Things Past,* and James' *The Golden Bowl* have all survived
without the grace of ready readability. If we are balked by works
like these, however, it is because our minds cannot keep up; there
is too much. In Miller's books, there is too little to keep the mind
nourished and awake: malnutrition, and not fatigue. Miller's
works are stretched with great deserts of *longeurs,* unshaped

visions and tedious, unintelligible preaching. "The air pockets, the alkali wastes" will leave the reader dried, distinterested, bored for chapters on end.

Henry Miller is obviously not for every reader. He is a difficult, deficient, and outrageous writer. He ought to be approached, if not with sympathy, at least with some awareness of what it is he is trying to do. The fully achieved artistic experiences —the verbal mastery, the humor, the extended narratives, the imaginative visions—can be, when plucked from their surroundings, rich and satisfying enough. For those who are prepared, however, the really enlarging experience will be that of the man himself. There isn't likely to be such another.

THE LEGACY OF HENRY MILLER

Kingsley Widmer

Miller started, as it were, with an apocalyptic "kick in the pants" at the dubious and dying heroic verities. To fill the void left by the collapsed idealisms, he turned out a vast and miscellaneous steam of boozy egotistical verbiage which included a small stream of good iconoclastic and comic rhetoric. Where his pyrotechnical style and buffoonish gesturing come together, he produced, I believe, work of intrinsic merit. But when he played the self-grandizing fundamentalist of the imagination, he produced only the *blagueur* man of letters and the cornball literary saint. The wordy by-product of that effort, as a poet candidly put it, turns out to be "inspirational chats for semiliterate bohemians and rebels with 'C+' minds." [1] But our primary concern is with the writings of Miller, and not with his apparently ambiguous sociological and religious effects and with the personal therapy of Saint Henry. In Miller's case, we may take his word for it that the artist is the clown.

Another evaluation can be posed by considering the role of Millerian literature (not the role of Miller) amidst other Ameri-

---

1. Letter from Stewart Millpond to the author (July 17, 1960).

can writing.[2] *Tropic of Cancer* and its appendages, I have already
suggested, significantly belong with the idiosyncratic and rebellious poetic-prose testaments of Thoreau, Cummings, Agee, and
others—a native extension of European traditions of Varronian
satire and picaresque potpourri. On the other hand, Miller's major
purpose of self-discovery—*"l'homme que j'étais, je ne suis plus"*
(*Black Spring,* 39)—and all the autobiographical rumination and
burlesque that belong with this American-as-romantic-artist are
part of the pathetic immaturity of American literature.

The tradition of self-sentimental and wordy naïve exaltation
—best known in Sherwood Anderson, then self-parodying itself in
Thomas Wolfe, William Saroyan, Jack Kerouac, and a host of
lesser writers—may be the major tradition of American prose,
quantitatively speaking, and the murky edge of the European
Bildungsroman and the quasi-literature of confession and case
history. In Miller, the confessional strain crosses, though not for
the first time, with the vast sub-literature of homemade metaphysics and millennial exhortation which we find in the native
radicalism of nineteenth-century American utopians, and in its
predecessors, the antinomian tracts of seventeenth-century English
Protestantism. But Miller, lacking demonic rigor and too patently
the indulgent personal and artistic sybarite, is no major heretic.
The garrulous American littérateur takes on an emphatically
buffoonish cast when playing the rebel as well as when supposedly
baring an anguished soul.[3]

When we relate Miller to the contemporary American literary
scene, some effect on the literary rebels of the 1950's, the "Beats,"
seems evident, Lawrence Ferlinghetti appropriately borrowed a
Miller title to label his collection of comic-pastiche verses, *A*

---

2. Charles Glisksburg takes Miller as representing an apocalyptic school
of social rebellion, anti-politics, and individualism running from D. H. Lawrence through Dylan Thomas ["Literature and Society," *The Arizona Quarterly,* VIII (Summer, 1952), 138]. Miller's origins are not so Anglo-Saxon as
this article would seem to suggest.

3. A rather left-handed praise of Miller by intellectuals is fairly
common. Miller at his best, writes Seymour Krim, gives a "vivid experience
of what shapeless modern existence could become" ["The Netherworld of
Henry Miller," *Commonweal* LVII (October 24, 1952), 271].

Coney Island of the Mind.[4] Miller is a possible source as well as an admirer of the swelling and embracing "bop" prose of the confessional literary "saint," Jack Kerouac.[5] Possibly from Miller, but more likely translated from similar surrealist sources, come the epithets of incongruity and the fractured invective which provide the major stylistic distinction of such "Beat" poets as Allen Ginsberg and Gregory Corso. Miller's rhetorical gestures may be his main "influence," though certainly the personal fragmentation and the stylization of the obscene in his confessions have provided a standard for ornate "daring" and for strident confusion in the more literary mode of self-exposure, as in William Borrough's *Naked Lunch.* But at their best the Beats also follow Miller in grotesque comedy of defiance.[6]

More generally, and perhaps more significantly, Miller importantly contributed to the increasing dominant and major poetic-naturalistic American styles—surreal, obscene, fantastic, iconoclastic, learned, colloquial, lavish, and desperate—which, in their mixing of low and high elements, provide an increased richness of language and awareness. Put another way, Miller's work—especially his early writings—have provided *ground* for such poetic-fantastic comedies of alienation as Algren's *A Walk on the Wild Side,* Ellison's *Invisible Man,* Bellow's *Henderson the Rain King,* and Heller's *Catch-22.* Miller's violent fantasies also appear to be having some direct effect on the early 1960's writing of Norman Mailer. And critics have rightly noted that a delightful bawdy comedy of American rebelliousness abroad, J. P. Donleavy's *The Ginger Man,* belongs to the *Tropic of Cancer* tradition of

---

4. Such rhetorical gestures have their own tradition. I recall that in some piece or other written in the 1920's, Maxwell Bodenheim, the archetypal Greenwich Villager and destructive bohemian, spoke of "the Coney Island of the soul." "Strange Artistic Sophistication of America," *Four Quarters,* XI (Nov., 1961).

5. See Miller's preface to Jack Kerouac, *The Subterraneans* (New York, 1959), pp. 5-7. Kerouac, of course, is indebted to Miller in another sense in following out his fractured life-style, including an attempted withdrawal to *Big Sur.* See his 1962 novel of that title.

6. For a discussion of the relevant tradition, see my "The Literary Rebel," *Centennial Review,* VI (Spring, 1962) and "The American Road," *University of Kansas City Review,* XXVI (Summer, 1960).

wild nihilistic humor.[7] Miller's best work partakes of this major direction or our literature—the sardonic, physical, rebellious, and expansive tradition of American comedy.[8]

For Miller's intrinsic merit as well as his significant contribution is in extreme comedy. Rational and moral comedy, the historians tell us, used society and its common sense as a norm to make the comic standard a golden mean. Irrational and amoral comedy, as with Millerian frenzy and bemused alienation, uses the sense of loss of authenticity and community as its fractured norm, and so instead of a golden mean we get a black extreme of humor. For much of twentieth-century experience, Miller may well belong to the more relevant comic mode.

The twentieth-century arts of defying despair take several directions; one is into comic rhetoric, as in the late Joyce and other self-propelled verbal machines, in psychoanalytic complete verbalization of recall, and in surrealism's absolute release of language and imagery from convention and logic. To this rhetorical comedy, Miller adds a colloquial looseness (and prolixity), a grandiose sentimentality (and paucity of rigor), and a naïve egotism (and self-alienation) which seem peculiarly American. Patently,

---

7. I have, of course, omitted Miller's influence and role outside of America. *The Black Book,* by Miller's best-known protege, Lawrence Durrell, is a rather self-consciously rococo adaptation of *Cancer,* and of low-life confession, rhetorical cadenzas, uterine imagery, and labyrinthine poses. It lacks the defiance and exuberance of Miller's best writing.

8. Miller again attempts a comic literary form in *Just Wild About Harry* (New York, 1963), a somewhat derivative and forced "antidrama." Drawing on Ionesco, Saroyan, Sartre (*No Exit* seems the basis for the final, and most interesting, scene), he also draws heavily on stock Miller material: the golden-hearted whore, the young "innocent" girl, the Brooklyn boy thug-pimp (Harry), and a number of minor vaudeville types (a dwarf, a German in long winter underwear, a blindman, a double-talking doctor, etc.). The theme is grossly sentimental, and tough-guy Harry really does love the innocent girl in the end—love is all. There are several nice iconoclastic bits, such as Harry's long (and completely out of character) common-sense polemic against "the bomb" (pp. 125-26). There is an endless amount of stage business—occasionally suggestive but mostly excessive and imposed nostalgic folderol from ancient vaudeville. The play, in the anti-theater tradition, jokes about itself, but not very humorously, and certainly not enough to cover up the embarrassment of its sloppy development, flat dialogue and mawkish "ideas."

the heroic epic and tragedy are not likely for these times. The large novel of the morals and manners of a viable and multi-dimensional society necessarily seems vestigial. The discordant lyric the aslant picaresque, the personal revery, the satiric apocalypse, and, especially, grotesque poetic comedy seem the most likely and responsive forms for the present. Thus I suggest that, while Miller is a minor writer, he may—in his work—have a major relevance.

One of Miller's silly bemusements is to preen himself before the mirror of an imagined future and see that great guy and artist Henry Miller being admired by posterity. However, Miller may have already reached his greatest popular and critical reputations —given a boost by the censorship furor—considering that his reputation must bear the burden of an immense amount of bad writing. Even leaving that aside, Miller at his best is limited in scope, experience, imaginative form, insight, human types, range of feeling, intelligence, and gesture; in short, he is a minor writer. This is not intended as simple denigration but just as an indication that it would be specious to discuss his work as if it were fulfilled and fulfilling, a major style and attitude in itself, a primary force and form of sensibility. To the degree that Miller found himself, it was by a commitment to the grotesque and marginal; both a strength and a weakness, his oddity must remain his definition. Naturally, to predict what the future will do with him, as a means of evaluation, is dangerous; literary history is probably no more honest and wise than the rest of history. We need not, then, seri-ously locate his place in some American factory-style literary pan-theon, even though it is mostly filled with anomalous and weird writers with whom Miller would be at home.

Miller's main creation, I suggest, is the rhetoric of grotes-querie. In a sense there is little behind his rhetoric—not much dramatic world of autonomous characters and patterns, not any major moral or social engagement, and not a unique way of knowledge or of life-style. His distinctive quality may be the Americanization of the literature of the absolute rebellion in which defiance is modified by bumptiousness, bombast by candor, extremity be geniality, nastiness by earnestness, and so on. In short, Miller's American ordinariness does qualify him from the extreme explorers of sensibility; he is a buffoonish version of the great tradition. The mindloose and fancy-wild American talker, he transcends the fatally ordinary family, ethos, and self—and our perplexing, threatening, and dubious world—by his eloquent and grandiloquent gestures. Miller's rhetoric becomes his one identity, hiding as well as holding his irregular insights.

His words exaggerate all, including his own foolishness; and thus he achieves the basic principle of buffoonery. Such a role has its own poignant assertion, but it most displays, as do every one of his portraits and self-portraits, the loss of all authentic heroism. His figures lack almost all tragic, moral, and organic consciousness. Miller, of course, is a bit of a fraud about his comic nihilism, declaiming all sorts of artistic, social and religious values. His poses as artist and saint, while hardly vicious, do not need to be taken very seriously. In a way more willynilly than a great artist or person, Miller testifies effectively to the loss of values, to a drastically incomplete humanity, to the anti-heroism so pervasive in our genuine literature. Such grotesqueness has its profound truths in a world in which individuality is increasingly marginal and heroic patterns increasingly gratuitous. Adventure into a closed world and rebellion against amorphous doom are obviously foolish. But the Millerian grotesque makes the rhetorical gestures of adventure, and he rebels by refusing heroic poses as well as victimization. Thus to insist on one's grotesqueness is to insist on one's being—a residual, invert, yet finally crucial heroism.

The buffoon is often a desperate and sly rebel. The more serious his poses, the more absurd he seems—is this why, knowingly or not, Miller plays at the most gigantic roles of great artist and prophet and saint and unique human being and god? While such buffoonery must be of ancient lineage, it is hard to recall anyone else quite so exhaustively playing the role as self-important writer. It must be granted that one curious interest Miller has is that he puts into books hundreds of thousands of bombastic, ruminative, casual, pretentious, disorderly, foolish words which have not usually been put into books at all. While the result is occasionally striking, but more often tedious, such literary buffoonery has a salutary charm and poignance. Especially poignance, for when we turn from Miller to many pretentious confessions and prophecies and art, they justly appear weak. The wisdom of the buffoon is to swell himself up until we see him, and everything else, in true proportion. Miller is also a symptomatic American, as ordinary man and literary rhetorician; he is so far "outside," as it were, that he stands revealed as a central image of our peculiarity.

Miller's best writing and most original gestures also result in grotesquely humorous catharsis. The rebel-buffoon's one heroism is his own defiant absurdity, and his reflection of it in others, as he dances in his torn rhetoric. Miller's verbal comedy, his one achieved art, is ragged but responsively open. It provides a legacy of motley for other rebel-buffoons, and for more sardonic comedians. The topsy-turvy gesture is all; but it is sufficient to be a suggestive and amusing affirmation of the lively human.

ALIENATION AND REBELLION
TO NOWHERE:
EXISTENTIALISM AND ALIENATION
IN AMERICAN LITERATURE

Sidney Finkelstein

A direct link between the two generations of "disillusion," that which followed the First World War and that which followed the Second, is provided by Henry Miller. For while he is of the generation of Fitzgerald, Eliot, Faulkner and Dos Passos, he did not burst into the broad American literary consciousness until the late 1950's and early 1960's. His books like *Tropic of Cancer* (1934)[1] and *Tropic of Capricorn* (1939)[2] had been barred from publication or sale in the United States as pornography. The lifting of the ban generated tremendous literary excitement, the books becoming best-sellers and Miller being praised by otherwise responsible critics as one of the greatest of living writers.

The excitement was not solely one of belated discovery. The form that Miller's "revolt" took, as one of the "disillusioned" after the First World War, was much like that of the self-named

---

1. Miller, Henry, *Tropic of Cancer* (Grove, N.Y., 1961).
2. Miller, *Tropic of Capricorn* (Grove, N.Y., 1961).

"beat generation" after the Second World War. It was as much a way of life as a way of writing, a defiant, vituperative resignation from society with the writing serving as an autobiographical manifesto for his behavior.

Born in 1891, Miller was reared in Brooklyn, N.Y., and supported himself by various odd jobs until 1924, when he decided to devote himself to writing. In 1930 he made Paris his home, writing while struggling against hunger and poverty, and returned to the United States after the war broke out, in 1940.

The pathos of impotence underlies the bravado of Henry Miller's declaration of war against the whole world, and is admitted in the utter, self-revelatory frankness with which he writes. Perhaps we cannot quite call it impotence, because he did produce a series of books. But there is a tacit surrender in their formlessness, raising seriously the question of what permanence they might have beyond their impact as "sensations." The process of organizing experience into an art form involves a certain minimum of self-criticism, which in the big artists becomes the ability to get out of their own skin and embrace a sweep of life. Miller, however, relies wholly on his remarkable "gift for gab." We think of the kind of book we might have gotten had there been a real Don Quixote, and instead of Cervantes' narrative, we had only the diary of the brave if addle-headed Don.

Miller tries to put a good face on his surrender. He says, "I have made a silent compact with myself not to change a line of what I write." Turgenev and Dostoievsky had their perfection, "but in Van Gogh's letters there is a perfection beyond either of these. It is the triumph of the individual over art." But Van Gogh did not substitute writing letters for painting pictures, and the letters are those of a man engaged in a successful, if harrowing, struggle to create solid works of art. Yet here too Miller strikes a note that would resound in the 1960's, and not only in literature but also in painting and music, as in the derisive joking of "pop art" and in "indeterminate" music. The artist sacrifices his future to the impact of the moment, and the underlying thought is, if the world has no future, why worry about the future of an art work?

What is Miller's "triumph"? He reiterates that he has renounced the bondage to a demanding world, and has found freedom. "I don't ask to go back to America, to be put in double harness again, to work the treadmill. No, I prefer to be a poor man of Europe. God knows, I am poor enough; it only remains to be a man." This is in *Tropic of Cancer*. Shortly after, we learn that his dubious "freedom" involves ghost-writing theses for incompetent writers, and composing publicity pamphlets for a house of prostitution.

To be free of society is to be free like an animal. The animal can go where it wants but is everywhere prey to hunger and enemies. Miller glimpses this. "I made up my mind that I would hold on to nothing, that I would expect nothing, that henceforth I would live as an animal, a beast of prey, a rover, a plunderer. Even if war were declared, and it were my lot to go, I would grab the bayonet and plunge it, plunge it up to the hilt." He makes love like an animal, and bravely describes it down to the last clinical detail. This is his battle against society, against the prudes and philistines. But it is also his surrender to a loss of humanity. For to see a woman as more than an immediate sex object, to see her as a human being with her own needs, is to become involved, to acknowledge demands on oneself. Miller wants human relationships but is afraid to pay the price, and so declaims in justification, "People are like lice—they get under your skin and bury themselves there. You scratch and scratch until the blood comes, but you can't get permanently deloused."

Whatever permanence Miller's art may lack, it is certainly significant as a social phenomenon and "type response" of our times. For Miller's was one that many others were making, and would make in the 50's more than the 30's. It is that one must renounce society in order to gain one's own humanity. And the value of his frankness is that we can find in his books—if we look—how humanity shrinks in these terms. His heart will go out to a beggar, a prostitute, a sick dog. Thus, he finds in himself love for humanity and asserts his own. But he can learn of massacres, mass starvation, disasters elsewhere, not under his nose, and he gloats that he remains unmoved. "I am inoculated against every disease, every calamity, every sorrow and misery. It's the culmination of a life of fortitude." But this "fortitude" is a calculated self-centredness, which he can only justify by claiming that all the world is equally bestial, and he alone has the courage to say so. What he also reveals is the anguish in which this leaves him. In *Tropic of Capricorn* he cries, "Now it dawns on me with full clarity: *you are alone in the world.*" It is bitter to be alone. And again in *Tropic of Cancer,* he cries, "My world of human beings had perished; I was utterly alone in the world and for friends I had the streets, and the streets spoke to me in that sad, bitter language compounded of human misery, yearning, regret, failure, wasted effort."

To really live is to live in the world that includes society. The more a person cuts himself off from any knowledge of it, the more he renounces it, the more irrational and frightful are the blows it delivers. Miller fights back by cursing it. Realizing, perhaps unconsciously, the impotence of such a verbal attack, he bolsters the words with violence and every obscene insult in his vocabulary. "The world needs to be blown to smithereens." And again, in *Tropic of Capricorn,* "I want to annihilate the whole earth. It's a huge piece of stale cheese with maggots festering inside it. F--- it! Blow it to hell! Kill, kill, kill: Kill them all, Jews and Gentiles, young and old, good and bad. . . ."

Like an existentialist—Miller comes as close as one can to existentialism without using the terminology—he cannot refrain from sweeping generalizations about history, making a virtue out of his ignorance. Napoleon was "the last big man of Europe." Or he will suddenly fall in love with primitive society and the middle ages. There was a "glorious light" in the land, he says, and "then came the scientific age and darkness fell over the land"—the darkness in Miller's mind, his retreat into infantilism. It prevents him from seeing what beacon lights of human strivings and progress there are in the world along with the evils he so vituperatively reports, and it blights the poet in him.

Miller the poet is bright, sensitive, curious, observant, full of vitality, and the pity is that Miller the mind gives the poet so little to work with. He swings between a passionate welcome to life and furious revulsion against it, between a humanized and an alienated response to the same object. He can present beautiful, humanized portrayals of Paris. "Indigo sky swept clear of fleecy clouds, gaunt trees infinitely extended, their black boughs gesticulating like a sleepwalker." And again:

> The rain had stopped and the sun breaking through the soapy clouds touched the glistening rubble of roofs with a cold fire. I recall now how the driver leaned out and looked up the river toward Passy way. Such a healthy, simple approving glance, as if he were saying to himself: "Ah, spring is coming! And God knows, when spring comes to Paris the humblest mortal alive must feel that he dwells in paradise. But it was not only this—it was the intimacy with which his eyes rested upon the scene. It was *his* Paris.

And the same Paris can be presented in the most alienated light. "Paris is like a whore." And again:

> In the blue of an electric dawn the peanut shells look wan and crumpled; along the beach at Montparnasse the water lilies bend and break. When the tide is on the ebb and only a few syphilitic mermaids are left stranded in the muck, the Dome looks like a shooting gallery that's been struck by a cyclone. Everything is slowly dribbling back to the sewer. For about an hour there is a deathlike calm during which the vomit is mopped up. Suddenly the trees begin to screech. . . . The moment has come to void the last bagful of urine. The day is sneaking in like a leper.

It is a different kind of alienated vision from Eliot's, Faulkner's or Dos Passos'. Miller's alienation is a weapon of attack and defense, part of the war fights, in the course of which he must consciously constrict his own humanity. He hurls his words connoting sex, dirt, disease and drains like a small boy hurling mud balls at the wall of a school building. It is a strange revolt for "freedom," which leaves him incessantly plucking off the tentacles that the world he renounces keeps laying on him.

What brings Miller to an existentialist position is his search for some human basis for living, which he can assert in the face of a world he regards as inimical and absurd. If he is not an existentialist, this is only because it is an explicit philosophy and he does not bother with philosophies. In *The Colossus of Maroussi*,[3] written in 1940, describing his visit to Greece, he expresses the existentialist view very succinctly. A Frenchwoman, wife of a shopkeeper, annoys him with her remarks in favor of civilization, and out comes his stream of vituperation:

> *Madame,* I am thinking of you now, of that sweet and fetid stench of the past which you throw off. . . . You are the black satin ghost of everything which refuses to die a natural death. . . . You are the white of a rotten egg. You stink.
>
> Madam, there are always two paths to take: one back toward the comforts and security of death, the other forward to nowhere.

"Forward to nowhere" is the key phrase. It also summarizes Miller's "rebellion," and the "rebellion" of the "beat generation" of writers in the 1950's, who hailed Miller as their spiritual godfather. Around such figures the shallow concept has been propagated of the artist as perpetual rebel, asserting the perpetual "nonconformisim" of art.

The truth is that rebellions are made in real life, not in art. They occur when conditions for the mass of people become intolerable, and the institutions under which they live, instead of assisting their progress, stifle it. What art has done is progressively to humanize the world and the relations among people in it; to make men aware of their own potentialities, to reveal the path-

---

3. Miller, *The Colossus of Maroussi* (New Directions, N.Y., 1941).

ways for many-sided growth and expose the destructive forces that impede this growth. Its main line of achievement has thus ever been on the side of the forces for freedom and progress. In this sense, we can call the artist a "rebel," but the rebellion is not outside society. Rather, it puts the artist in close relations to the forces in society making for forward movement. To see art as "permanent rebellion" is to place the artist in permanent alienation from his fellow human beings. It undermines the potentialities of art itself, by constricting the artist's own humanity. Alienated art is still art, but it is art announcing its own imminent death.

The fact that an art which prides itself on its "permanent rebellion" and on thumbing its nose at society, is honored, praised and rewarded by this very society, where any criticism of its real exploitive relations is looked upon as dangerous and even treasonable, indicates how empty this show of rebellion is. When those who uphold the status quo cannot pretend that it offers any vistas of human progress, they can be quite satisfied with a "rebellion" that reviles it but marches "forward to nowhere." Yet there is a kind of abject admission of its own despair in itself that society shows in the praise and even acclaim it gives to writers like Henry Miller and his numerous progeny of the 1950's. For what these writers can be described as doing, figuratively, in their gloating naturalism of coition, perversion, toilet, drug addiction and mental and bodily dissolution, is forcing this society to eat its own excrement, as if to admit that this is its truth.

Perhaps the book that can best be cited, if not admired, as a classic example is William Burroughs' *Naked Lunch* (1959).[4] Where Henry Miller's rambling at least showed him and people he met in some open-air and real-life surroundings, the "stream of talk" of this book takes the form of the fantasy-stream-of-consciousness of a narcotics addict. It achieves a brutal humor in its portrayal of how the mind and body can destroy themselves, doing this with such intensity that to read it becomes a kind of training in masochism. It makes some gestures at an attack upon political reaction, with the content of a boy thumbing his nose or derisively

4. Burroughs, William, *Naked Lunch* (Grove, N.Y., 1959).

opening his fly. It abounds of course in intensely alienated imagery: "Smell of chili houses and dank overcoats and atrophied testicles. . . . A heaving sea of air hammers in the purple brown dusk tainted with rotten metal smell of sewer gas." The author is talented. One of the characteristics, however, of this talent which dwells in alienation is that each successive writer makes his predecessor look like a noble figure, even an esteemed classic. Thus compared to William Burroughs, even Henry Miller appears to be a humanist.

THE PITCHING OF LOVE'S MANSION
IN THE *TROPICS* OF HENRY MILLER

Alan Friedman

More than any other year, 1926 climaxed the era of the so-called "Lost Generation" of American expatriate writers, although by then almost all their important documents, from Sherwood Anderson's *Winesburg Ohio* in 1919 to F. Scott Fitzgerald's *The Great Gatsby* in 1925, had already been written, published, and received. The year 1926 was climactic, however, since that year was Hemingway's—it was the year of *The Sun Also Rises* and it was the last of the *Moveable Feast* years—and Hemingway, despite his subsequent repudiation of Gertrude Stein's "dirty, easy labels," [1] has come to epitomize the writers of his era, the writers we still glibly label "the Lost Generation."

Henry Miller, in 1926, was still in America, though he was "of" America far less than any of his self-exiled compatriots; for with the exception of the very early years, when he was growing up in Brooklyn, and the late years, when he was settled in his Big Sur Paradise, Miller has been consistently vehement in his

---

1. Ernest Hemingway, *A Moveable Feast: Sketches of the Author's Life in Paris in the Twenties* (New York: Charles Scribner's Sons, 1964), p. 31.

opposition to everything he sees America symbolizing. "I can think of no street in America," he writes in *Tropic of Capricorn,*

> or of people inhabiting such a street, capable of leading one on toward the discovery of the self. I have walked the streets in many countries of the world but nowhere have I felt so degraded and humiliated as in America. I think of all the streets in America combined as forming a huge cesspool, a cesspool of the spirit in which everything is sucked down and drained away. . . . Over this cesspool the spirit of work weaves a magic wand, palaces and factories spring up side by side, and munition plants and chemical works and steel mills and sanatoriums and prisons and insane asylums. The whole continent is a nightmare producing the greatest misery of the greatest number. I was one, a single entity in the midst of the greatest jamboree of wealth and happiness (statistical wealth, statistical happiness) but I never met a man who was truly wealthy or truly happy.[2]

And elsewhere he expresses his fears of America's influence on the entire world: "I see America spreading disaster," he writes, "'I see America as a black curse upon the world. I see a long night settling in and that mushroom which has poisoned the world withering at the roots." [3]

But by 1926 Miller had yet to discover Paris, the Paris where, as he puts it, he was to be "born and reborn over and over. Born while walking the streets, born which sitting in a cafe, born while lying over a whore. Born and reborn again and again" (*Black Spring*, p. 161). In 1926 Miller was not only still in America, still unknown and still spiritually isolated, but he was

---

2. Henry Miller, *Tropic of Capricorn* (New York: Grove Press, Inc., 1961), p. 12; hereafter *Capricorn.*

3. Henry Miller, *Black Spring* (New York: Grove Press, Inc., 1963), p. 21; hereafter cited in the text.

already thirty-five—nearly a decade older than Hemingway—and he was just beginning to write full time. Up to this point he had written, in addition to a series of prose-poems he attempted to sell from door to door, a single still-unpublished novel, and he was to produce two more before his fourth, *Tropic of Cancer,* was finally published, in Paris, in 1934.

Thus, although for the next quarter of a century he remained a kind of writer non grata in England and America, Miller the artist and Miller the cause had been simultaneously born, and born, it should be noted, to the sound of trumpets and a hallelujah chorus. Here, for instance, is Lawrence Durrell, one of the many early hymnists, hailing *Tropic of Cancer:*

> It strikes me as being the only really man-size piece of work which the century can really boast of. It's a howling triumph from the word go; and not only is it a literary and artistic smack on the bell for everyone, but it really gets down on paper the blood and bowels of our time. I have never read anything like it. I did not imagine anything like it could be written; and yet, curiosuly, reading it I seemed to recognize it as something which I knew we were all ready for. The space was all cleared for it. *Tropic* turns the corner into a new life which has regained its bowels. In the face of it eulogy becomes platitude. . . . I love its guts. I love to see the canons of oblique and pretty emotion mopped up; to see every whim-wham and bagatelle of your contemporaries from Eliot to Joyce dunged under. God give us young men the guts to plant the daisies on top and finish the job.[4]

Granted, Durrell was only twenty-two at the time, and might not be expected to know any better, but, with almost undeviating con-

<hr>

4. Lawrence Durrell, in Lawrence Durrell and Henry Miller, *A Private Correspondence*, ed. George Wickes (New York: E. P. Dutton & Co., 1963), p. 4.

sistency, such self-indulgent hyperbole has characterized his view of Miller ever since—and it has become an increasingly typical attitude as more and more voices have blended in an uncritical hailing of Miller's supreme significance.

But if Miller enthusiasts have tended to view him as a cause, as a banner around which they could rally in eager defiance of all the authoritarian taboos they glibly associate with Anglo-Saxon society, at least they have not gone the way of his equally vehement detractors who completely ignored the artist for the cause. For instance, according to Elmer Gertz, the trial lawyer who successfully defended *Tropic of Cancer* in Chicago, the self-righteous California judges who had earlier ruled Miller's two *Tropic* books obscene, "presumed to pass upon the character, or the morals, of Miller, the unorthodox ideas that outraged them, his sexual explicitness, and the use of four-letter words of Anglo-Saxon origin, and they gave little credence to the literary experts who held the *Tropic* books in high esteem." [5] In writing of the landmark Chicago trial of *Cancer,* Hoke Norris has noted that time and again either hearsay or a quick glance at a page or two of the book was enough for the self-appointed guardians of community morality. "This sort of instantaneous literary and judicial judgment," he writes, "is to be found throughout the case, not only among police officials but also among some newspaper columnists, clergyman, and the writers of wrathful letters." [6]

Norris goes on to cite various police actions against the book, as well as statements by the police chiefs involved; the following case is typical. One captain, the acting chief of a Chicago suburb, was asked if he believed he was enforcing the state obscenity law when, without a warrant and on his own initiative, he pressured local booksellers into removing *Tropic of Cancer* from their shelves." 'No, I wouldn't say the state law,' replied Captain Morris. 'We were just enforcing a moral law which I believe has a place in a town such as ours where we have good,

---

5. Elmer Gertz, "Henry Miller and the Law," in *Henry Miller and the Critics,* ed. George Wickes (Carbondale: Southern Illinois University Press, 1963), p. 181; hereafter *Critics.*

6. Hoke Norris, " 'Cancer' in Chicago," reprinted from *Evergreen Review,* No. 25, p. 5.

religious people and many churches.' " [7] The full implications of such a statement are truly frightening to contemplate.

For many of us in the English-speaking world, then, the name Henry Miller conjures up thoughts of a more or less noble crusade against proper Bostonians and their ilk throughout the land; for, despite the hopes of Miller and his many fervent supporters, he has gained a reputation in his native country based not primarily on widespread recognition of his uncommon genius, but rather on his ability to rouse the shocked sensibilities of some and the civil libertarianism of others. The censorship war, of course, has been going on at least since the time of Plato, who feared the influence of the poets on his young Guardians, and it seems likely to continue a good while longer. In 1933, in response to Judge Woolsey's now historic decision on Joyce's *Ulysses,* Morris Ernst wrote that "the *Ulysses* case marks a turning point. It is a body-blow for the censors. The necessity of hypocrisy and circumlocution in literature has been eliminated. Writers need no longer seek refuge in euphemisms. They may describe basic human functions without fear of the law. . . . Under the *Ulysses* case it should henceforth be impossible for the censors legally to sustain an attack against any book of artistic integrity, no matter how frank and forthright it may be. We have travelled a long way from the days of Bowdler and Mrs. Grundy and Comstock. We may well rejoice over the result." [8] Unfortunately, in the afterglow of victory, Ernst mistook a single battle for the entire war— a war in which we have since witnessed the battles of *Lady Chatterley's Lover,* of *Fanny Hill,* of *Tropic of Cancer,* a war, in fact, which is far from ended. The Marquis de Sade, to mention only the most obvious, still looms in the future, as does perhaps a third of Miller's published writings.

One must assume, especially considering the many remarkable opinions written by various courts in the last few years, that the war is being won—and it need detain us no further. Still, it does warrant our consideration since Miller the cause—a Miller

---

7. Hoke Norris, " 'Cancer' in Chicago," reprinted from *Evergreen Review,* No. 25, p. 8.
8. Morris L. Ernst, "Forward" to *Ulysses,* by James Joyce (New York: The Modern Library, 1946), pp. vii-viii.

obviously noble, obviously on the side of the angels—tends to become inextricable from Miller the artist, a figure of still questionable stature. Stanley Kauffmann, in one of the most balanced reviews of *Cancer,* focuses on just this problem in considering the inflated praise the book has evoked. "I hazard a couple of guesses at extrinsic reasons for this," he writes. "First, when a gifted man writes a prosecutable book, it is often over-lauded as a tactical move by those interested in the freedom of letters—especially those who hold that sex is Beautiful, not sexy. Second, possibly these statements are, as much as anything else, a tribute to Miller's purity of commitment, to his abhorrence of the pietisms of Literature and the proprieties of the Literary Life, to his willingness—if not downright eagerness—to suffer for the right to live and write as he chooses. His is no small spirit," Kauffmann concludes, "it is just not as large as some have told us." [9]

Let us, then, examine that spirit Miller offers us in his early fiction, *Tropic of Cancer, Black Spring,* and *Tropic of Capricorn,* focusing primarily on *Cancer,* the first, most important, and best of this loosely connected trilogy. Two prefatory points should be made before continuing, however. First, it should be noted that Miller is extremely difficult to quote in brief, for what most characterizes his writing—and represents both the best and the worst thing about it—is his interminable jamming together of formless, exuberant imagery. Miller, in fact, writes like a Spasmodic poet, seemingly afraid that words are going out of style and, unless he employs them all immediately, they will be lost to us forever.

Second is the question of whether these books are novels at all. Miller insists they are not, even to the point where he writes an outraged response to a highly favorable article by Edmund Wilson simply because the latter had assumed that *Cancer* is a work of fiction.

> Wilson praised Miller for his skilful ironic portrait of a particular kind of "vaporing" poseur, for making his hero really live, "and not merely in his vaporings or his poses. He gives us the genuine American bum come to lead the

9. Stanley Kauffmann, "An Old Shocker Comes Home," in *Critics,* p. 159.

beautiful life in Paris; and he lays him away forever in his
dope of Pernod and dreams." To all of this praise for irony,
Miller replied: [10]
The theme of the book, moreover, is not at all what Mr.
Wilson describes: the theme is myself, and the narrator,
or the hero, as (Wilson) puts it, is also myself . . . the narrator . . . is me, because I have painstakingly indicated
throughout the book that the hero is myself. I don't use
"heroes," incidentally, nor do I write novels. I am the
hero, and the book is myself.[11]

Wayne Booth, in his brilliant study of the novel, cites this exchange between Wilson and Miller as exemplifying the contemporary critic's dilemma when considering the crucial question of
distance between author and character, and he sympathizes with
Wilson for making a very natural error. But there is overwhelming
evidence that, despite Miller's protestations to the contrary, Wilson
is basically right and Booth wrong. In *Cancer,* for instance, the
protagonist writes that "I have made a silent compact with myself
not to change a line of what I write. I am not interested in perfecting my thoughts, nor my actions." [12] And yet the first draft
manuscript of *Cancer* was three times the length of the published
version, and three times Miller rewrote the book.[13] With regard to
his Chronology, a supposedly factual account of his life, Miller

---

10. Wayne C. Booth, *The Rhetoric of Fiction* (Chicago and London:
The University of Chicago Press, 1961), p. 367.

11. Henry Miller, in a letter to *The New Republic,* May 18, 1938, reprinted in *Critics,* p. 29.

12. Henry Miller, *Tropic of Cancer* (Paris: Obelisk Press, 1960), p. 20;
hereafter *Cancer.*

13. See, for example, the "Chronology," by Miller, for the year 1934,
printed in *The Best of Henry Miller,* ed. Lawrence Durrell (London, Mel-
bourne, and Toronto: Wm. Heinemann Ltd., 1960), p. 385; hereafter *Best.*
On p. 37 of the same book, Miller writes that *Cancer* "was written several
times and in many places—in Paris." Durrell tells us that *Cancer* "was dis-
tilled out of a colossal MS which I was lucky enough to read, and which
could not have been less than fifteen hundred pages long. It seemed to me
that there was enough material to make three or four *Tropic of Cancers*
from it" ("Studies in Genius: Henry Miller," in *Critics,* p. 105).

has said: "Here and there I'm deliberately putting down a lie—
just to throw the bastards off the track."[14]

The same, of course, goes for his "autobiographical romances," as he calls them—only more so. For instance, after
vividly detailing an extensive series of sexual conquests, the protagonist of *Capricorn* says: "It was going on this way all the time
even though every word I say is a lie" (190). Samuel Beckett, in a
perhaps apocryphal story, was asked if the title character of
Waiting for Godot was meant to be God. "Of course not," he
supposedly answered, "if I had meant God I would have said
God; I meant Godot." Whether the incident actually occurred
is beside the point; its moral remains loud, clear, and relevant:
be wary when an artist speaks of what he intended by his work.
Perhaps it would be best if, as E. M. Forster suggested, we read all
literature as though it were written in a single room, simultaneously and in effect, anonymously. In practice, however, we need
to strive for a satisfactory mean between the two extremes, especially when, as in Miller's case, author and protagonist have identical names and largely coextensive lives. As Kingsley Widmer, in
the best book to date on Miller, had noted, "it is unavoidable in
discussing Miller's work to call the central figure Henry Miller,
as does Henry Miller, though this is not a claim that the experiences are literal fact . . . in all probability Miller's writings about
Miller are not true, in several senses." [15]

These early books, then, with their loosely connected, anecdotal narrative, deal primarily with an alienated aging American
writer who divides his thoughts and energies between the intoxi-
cating life of Paris and the frenzied life of New York, and who
discovers that the world is essentially an uncongenial place for
such sensitive, personable individuals as himself. *Cancer's* similarities with *The Sun Also Rises* have been noted many times, as
for instance in this comment by Samuel Putnam, a cohort of

14. Quoted by Lawrence Durrell in *Art and Outrage: A Correspondence
about Henry Miller,* by Alfred Perles, Lawrence Durrell, and Henry Miller
(London: Putnam & Co., Ltd., 1959), p. 55.

15. Kingsley Widmer, *Henry Miller* (New York: Twayne Publishers, Inc.,
1963), p. 8.

Miller's in the early Paris days and also a minor character in *Cancer*: ". . . whatever may be said of Miller, he has summed up for us as no one else has the expatriates' Paris of the second phase: and I think it may be said that the *Tropic of Cancer* is to that phase what *The Sun Also Rises* is to the preceding one." [16] In addition, *Cancer* has affinities with *A Moveable Feast,* for both truly describe, to use Hemingway's words, "how Paris was in the early days when we were very poor and very happy." [17] For even though hungry, Hemingway tells us, the young, eager, in love, expatriate writer of the 1920's found Paris "a moveable feast." But by the time of *Cancer* the hopeful twenties have given way to the forlorn thirties, and the prototype of the hungry writer has become a middle-aged lecher making nihilistic gestures at all the old romantic shibboleths. And thus the causes of Miller's happiness are more complex and more obscure than Hemingway's, for the latter is young and the work is going well and he is generally satisfied with the world he inhabits. If in *his* early writings, Miller ultimately achieves an affirmation of sorts, it is an affirmation predicated upon despair, for one by one he has rejected all the traditional values, all the consolations conceived by other men and other artists. The very point of *Cancer,* in fact, as Mark Schorer has put it, "is that he has divested himself of every connection and responsibility in order to be free to do nothing but live with no money, no obligations, no residence, nothing except himself for life, and at that point he says, 'I am the happiest man in the world'." [18]

This world, Miller insists, is a cancerous zone, a hospital full of the dying and the deadly: "People are like lice," he says—"they get under your skin and bury themselves there. You scratch and scratch until the blood comes, but you can't get permanently deloused. Everywhere I go people are making a mess of their lives. Everyone has his private tragedy. It's in the blood now—misfortune, ennui, grief, suicide. The atmosphere is saturated

---

16. Samuel Putnam, "Henry Miller in Montparnasse," in *Critics*, p. 15.

17. Hemingway, *A Moveable Feast*, p. 211.

18. Mark Schorer, testifying in the case of "Commonwealth of Massachusetts vs. *Tropic of Cancer,*" printed in *Critics*, p. 162.

with disaster, frustration, futility" (21). And out of this misery
his imagination thus imposes upon others, emerges a perverse kind
of drunken glee, for "the effect upon me," he claims, "is ex-
hilarating. Instead of being discouraged, or depressed, I enjoy it.
I am crying for more and more disasters, for bigger calamities,
for grander failures. I want the whole world to be out of whack,
I want everyone to scratch himself to death" (21). What Miller
means, apparently, is that his spiritual malaise finds solace, even
delight, in an external despair at least as negative as the one
within.

In addition, *Tropic of Cancer* reads as a kind of scatological
Down and Out in Paris and London, for like the Orwell book, it
concerns the quest for food and shelter (among other things) during the days and nights of the Parisian Depression—only Orwell
seeks even the most menial and degrading work in order to survive at any cost; Miller, on the other hand, becomes a parasite in
order both to survive on his own terms (that is, without working)
and, despite his protestations to the contrary, in order to make
literature of the experience. At the beginning of *Cancer,* Miller
offers us a miniature portrait of the artist and his art.

> It is now the fall of my second year in Paris. I was sent here
> for a reason I have not yet been able to fathom. I have no
> money, no resources, no hopes. I am the happiest man
> alive. A year ago, six months ago, I thought that I was an
> artist. I no longer think about it, I *am.* Everything that
> was literature has fallen from me. There are no more
> books to be written, thank God. This then? This is not a
> book. This is libel, slander, defamation of character. This
> is not a book in the ordinary sense of the word. No, this is
> a prolonged insult, a gob of spit in the face of Art, a kick
> in the pants to God, Man, Destiny, Time, Love, Beauty
> . . . what you will. I am going to sing for you, a little off
> key perhaps, but I will sing. (11-12)

Art, then, becomes non-art, for it is not only formless and
eclectic, negative and destructive, but it serves for the artist not

as an end in itself but as a means to life. Elsewhere Miller writes that "art is only a stepping-stone to reality. It is the vestibule in which we undergo the rites of initiation. Man's task is to make of himself a work of art. The creations which man makes manifest have no validity in themselves; they serve to awaken." Consequently, he concludes, the artist must cease "immolating himself in his work," must cease creating out of a martyrdom "of sweat and agony. . . . We do not think of sweat and tears in connection with the universe; we think of joy and light, and above all of play." [19] And this is the kind of nay-saying which, since it is ultimately affirmative, we can readily accept—for even if art is not simply a spontaneously formed outpouring, even if art is not simply unrecollected and untranquilized emotion, it is pretty to talk as if it were.

Of Miller's semiautobiographical fiction, there are, to date, a total of nine excessively large volumes. They are unified primarily by similarities of mood and atmosphere, and only secondarily by subject matter, by, for instance, the dual theme of loss of innocence and initiation into manhood—an initiation which Miller's picaro has undergone enough times to become a fraternity unto himself. From time to time he renders this theme explicit, as when he discusses the effect upon himself of Henri Bergson's book, *Creative Evolution:* "When I think of the book now, and the way I approached it, I think of a man going through the rites of initiation. The disorientation and reorientation which comes with the initiation into any mystery is the most wonderful experience which it is possible to have" (Capricorn, p. 220). Nonetheless, and despite the rather earthy form such initiation usually takes in these writings, Miller's central concern in them "was not with sex . . . but with the problem of self-liberation." [20] Richard Ellmann, in testimony given during the Chicago trial of *Cancer,* expressed essentially the same view of that book when he said that "there is nothing which is attractive about sexuality

---

19. Henry Miller, "Of Art and the Future," from *Sunday After the War,* reprinted in *Best,* p. 237.

20. Henry Miller, in *The World of Sex,* reprinted in *Best,* p. 356. Miller is speaking specifically of *Cancer,* but the same holds for his other fiction.

as represented in it." Very much unlike, for example, *Fanny Hill*, a book which exalts sex, joyfully delighting in it and the life devoted to it, *Cancer* is rather "a criticism of life in Paris at that time and, by extension, a criticism of life throughout the world at that time." [21]

Miller's focal theme, and he expounds it at lengths sometimes painfully graphic, sometimes enormously funny, is disgust and revulsion at the stupidity and ugliness he sees all about him—and because his disgust and revulsion are both profoundly felt and often ineffectually transmuted into art, and because disease must, after all, be represented by disease, Miller rages on like a tidal wave of sewerage:

> If there were a man who dared to say all that he thought of this world, there would not be left him a square foot of ground to stand on. When a man appears the world bears down on him and breaks his back. There are always too many rotten pillars left standing, too much festering humanity for man to bloom. The superstructure is a lie and the foundation is a huge quaking fear. If at intervals of centuries there does appear a man with a desperate hungry look in his eye, a man who would turn the world upside down in order to create a new race, the love that he brings to the world is turned to bile and he becomes a scourge. . . . If any man ever dared to translate all that is in his heart, to put down what is really his experience, what is truly his truth, I think then the world would go to smash, that it would be blown to smithereens and no god, no accident, no will could ever again assemble the pieces. (240-241)

And because Miller would be this man and because he is a frustrated romantic whose vision of reality bears virtually no resemblance to the stagnant world he sees about him, his naïveté and

---

21. Richard Ellmann, quoted in " 'Cancer' in Chicago," pp. 14, 12.

his disillusionment give way, at times, to strident nihilism and profound despair. "I can't get it out of my mind," he says in *Cancer*, "what a discrepancy there is between ideas and living" (235). Nonetheless, the romanticism, the wide-eyed wonder of youthful innocence, not only clings but at times breaks forth into lyric passages of perhaps surprising beauty, as in the following passage from *Big Sur*, a much later book by a much mellower Miller:

> There were always birds: the pirates and scavengers of the blue as well as the migratory variety. (At intervals the condor passed, huge as an ocean liner.) Gay in plumage, their beaks were hard and cruel. They strung out across the horizon like arrows tied to an invisible string. In close they seemed content to dart, dip, swoop, careen. Some followed the cliffs and breakers, others sought the canyons, the gold-crested hills, the marble-topped peaks. . . . From the ocean depths there issued strange formations, contours unique and seductive. As if the Titans of the deep had labored for aeons to shape and mold the earth. Even millennia ago the great land birds were startled by the abrupt aspect of these risen shapes.[22]

Even as early as *Cancer*, however, the lyrical Miller is not only present, but present when we might expect him. Perhaps despite himself, his bubbling enthusiasm for life, for all of life, is self-infectious, and he continually breaks out in a hives-like joyfulness. Having written, "we're all dead, or dying, or about to die," he almost immediately refers to himself as "incurably optimistic! Still have one foot in the 19th century. I'm a bit retarded, like most Americans. . . . The mere thought of a meal— *another* meal—rejuvenates me. A meal! That means something to

22. Henry Miller, *Big Sur and the Oranges of Hieronymus Bosch* (New York: New Directions, 1957), p. 7.

go on—a few solid hours of work, an erection possibly. I don't deny it. I have health, good, solid, animal health. The only thing that stands between me and a future is a meal, *another* meal" (46, 55).

Food, in fact becomes *Cancer's* one transcending standard of value. Art may be an intrusion, love a diseased prostitution, and the world a rotting corpse, but food, that divine inspiration, is God's glory on earth. "Food," Miller writes with gusto, "is one of the things I enjoy tremendously" (13). And perhaps it is the only thing he enjoys tremendously always, for Miller, who often seems obsessed with the fact that he is not Jewish, adopts the traditionally Jewish belief in the therapeutic powers of food, in food as a nostrum for all the ills of life. Upon his long-delayed return to his parents' home in Brooklyn, a guilt-ridden Miller writes elsewhere, he feels a sudden compassion for the lower-middle-class sterility of their lives. But then, after the tears of this necessarily temporary reunion have been shed, the family turns, as usual, to the inevitable next meal. "The table was set; we were to eat in a few moments. It seemed natural that it should be thus, though I hadn't the slightest desire to eat. In the past the great emotional scenes which I had witnessed in the bosom of the family were nearly always associated with the table. We pass easily from sorrow to gluttony." [23]

The problem in *Cancer*, however, is far less likely to be that of gluttony than that of hunger. At one point, Miller's hunger becomes so acute that, despite his essentially passive, nonassertive nature, he feels constrained to initiate corrective action. Realizing "that no one would refuse a man a meal if only he had the courage to demand it," he writes to a dozen or so acquaintances, asking each the day of the week it would be convenient to have him come to dinner. Not only do none refuse him, but even those who can't stand him wine and dine him royally. "They were all obviously relieved," he writes, "when they realized that they would see me only once a week. And they were still more relieved when I said—'it won't be necessary any more.' They never asked

---

23. Henry Miller, "Reunion in Brooklyn," from *Sunday After the War,* reprinted in *Best,* p. 99.

why. They congratulated me, and that was all. Often the reason was I had found a better host; I could afford to scratch off the ones who were a pain in the ass" (60). Miller, for his part, never thinks to ask why his hosts do give him up so readily, but it is apparent that his feelings for them were mutual. Miller, however, continues blithely on. " 'Life,' he quotes Emerson as having said, 'consists in what a man is thinking all day.' If that be so," he adds, "then my life is nothing but a big intestine. I not only think about food all day, but I dream about it at night" (73).

But Miller's dreams and fantasies are as much sexual as they are gastronomical, and Paris serves equally well as caterer and procurer. "I have never seen a place like Paris," Miller comments, "for varieties of sexual provender" (160). And for the picaro of *Cancer,* life in Paris becomes, as much as anything else, an attempt to sample as much as possible of this so generously provided provender. The whorey hordes, like marching Chinamen four abreast, parade incessantly down the streets of Miller's cities—streets he associates, both literally and figuratively, with life in the raw and, therefore, with life unclothed in the devitalizing dehumanizing raiments worn by everyone who is not of the streets. As Miller puts it in *Black Spring:* "What is not in the open street is false, derived, that is to say, *literature.*" And he adds, "I was born in the street and raised in the street. . . . To be born in the street means to wander all your life, to be free" (1-3).

And thus Miller seeks out his whores, creatures of the street par excellence, and romanticizes them as fellow free spirits: Tania, with her "fat, heavy garters," her "soft, bulging thighs," "a Tania like a big seed, who scatters pollen everywhere," a Tania who is the loveliest Jew of them all, and for whose sake, Miller exclaims, "I too would become a Jew" (*Cancer,* pp. 13-15); Germaine, who bore all the obvious signs of her way of life (the boozy breath, the cheap jewelry, the rundown heels, the pasty rouge accentuating what it was meant to conceal), and yet like Molly Bloom exhibits in bed such an earthly joyousness—a joyousness clinically or cynically called nymphomania—that Miller quite naturally finds her delightful; and Claude, who, unlike Germaine, was not really cut out for this line of work, who was, at bottom, "just a good French girl of average breed and intelligence whom life had tricked somehow," and who "had a soul and a conscience . . . (and) refinement, too, which is bad—in a whore," and whom for a while Miller thought he loved (51).

There are, of course, innumerable others—enough in *Cancer* and *Capricorn* to people a street of brothels—and with a comic detachment, a saving irony of vision which is one of the outstanding features of Miller's writing, he records them all—the fat whores and the lean whores, the immoral and the amoral, the predatory, buzzardlike whores who are fundamentally man-haters and the merely hungry ones who, with both belly and bed warm and full, care nothing at all for a man's money. And because, like Yeats's ultrarational Crazy Jane, Miller can never forget that love has pitched its mansion in the place of excrement, his amatory encounters read like a series of experimental investigations into the accuracy of her assertion. Necessarily, Miller emphasizes those human organs, traditionally unmentionable and even at times unthinkable, which serve dual functions for Crazy Jane—and for everyone else. The duality is central when Carl, for whom Miller has been ghost-writing love letters for six months, at last goes to meet his rich, widowed correspondent. Although the lady is not only willing but downright eager, the luckless Carl spends the entire evening unable to find a delicate way of telling her that his bladder is full to bursting.

Later on in *Cancer,* when Miller gives us a description of Carl's room, he notes that "in the *bidet* were orange peels and the remnants of a ham sandwich" (227). The convenient and, in France, omnipresent *bidet* is, of course, the perfect symbol of the dual functioning of the sex organ, and Miller makes good use of it as when he rails at Claude's offensive delicacy. "Who wants a *delicate* whore!" he demands. "Claude would even ask you to turn your face away when she squatted over the *bidet!* All wrong! A man, when he's burning up with passion, wants to see things; he wants to see *everything,* even how they make water" (53).

The *bidet* also plays a key role subsequently when in a typical surrealistic flight of fancy, Miller imaginatively abstracts from his picaresque narrative and arrives at an existential epiphany in which, suddenly "inspired by the absolute hopelessness of everything," he envisages a new world where he can burrow fully and freely into life. As usual, he writes of the experience in terms of a symbolism both powerful and stridently abstruse:

> I made up my mind that I would hold on to nothing, that I would expect nothing, that henceforth I would live as an animal, a beast of prey, a rover, a plunderer. . . . At this very moment, in the quiet dawn of a new day was not the earth giddy with crime and distress? Had one single element of man's nature been altered, vitally, fundamentally altered, by the incessant march of history? . . . I have reached the limits of endurance. . . . The world which I have departed is a menagerie. The dawn is breaking on a new world, a jungle world in which the lean spirits roam with sharp claws. If I am a hyena I am a lean and hungry one: I go forth to fatten myself. (100-101)

All this quasi-mystical self-aggrandizing is as much pompous posturing for an effect as it is a serious attempt to find proper expression for an ever-recurring sense of hopelessness. But then, considering Miller's point of departure, what else could we expect? The scene Miller had been describing occurs, not surprisingly, in, a brothel where, perhaps despite his better judgment, he had conducted a rather dandified and panting disciple of Gandhi's. The young Hindu, despite his eagerness, is obviously out of his depth. Turning his head away and blushing violently, he asks Miller to do the choosing from among the "bevy of naked women" surrounding them. Then, in an awkward violation of decorum, he has Miller switch girls with him. Finally, he commits the ultimate *"faux pas"* in confusing the functions of the *bidet* and the toilet—and it is the resultant unflushable mess which actuates Miller's readily stimulated imagination, for he freely associates it not merely with his erstwhile companion, but with all disciples of any faith, and hence with all man's hopes for a better life either in this world or in the next. Miller believes not only that things are rotten, but that they are bound to get a good deal worse. And thus his incessant wallowing in filth and degradation, the so-called seamier aspects of life, as a kind of objective correlative for his despair.

One of the would-be burners of *Cancer* has said that it is "like a slut walking down a neighborhood street, half undressed and spewing filth to those near her," and that it "deals heavily with carnal experiences, with perversion, with human filth and excrement." [24] Deal with these things it does, of course, yet such a statement is misleading. For one thing, sexual perversion occurs rarely in Miller's fiction (unlike, for instance, Lawrence Durrell in his never-banned *Alexandria Quartet,* Miller is not fascinated by incest and homosexuality). At one point in *Cancer* he even expresses revulsion at a friend's espousal of masturbation, and in *Capricorn,* describing a boyhood attack on a sissy of a choirboy, he says, "it was a disgraceful performance, but it made us feel good. Nobody knew yet what a fairy was, but whatever it was we were against it" (135).

Even his seemingly endless pursuit of females—or, more precisely, of the sex organs of prostitutes—must be examined in context; for, although obviously obsessed with the "idea" of sex, Miller, especially in *Cancer,* is largely indifferent to it in reality. Despite his concern with his physical needs, he almost never goes out of his way to satisfy them. Taking a woman to bed—although he does so at every opportunity—seems always to be someone else's idea: the various women who accost him in the streets or the cafes, the blushing Hindu afraid to go upstairs alone, the friend who offers him the loan of his own latest bed-mate. Miller's reaction to the latter is typical: "I didn't know whether I wanted to or not," he says, but of course he does (279). It is free, it is convenient, and besides it saves him the cost of a night's lodging.

Miller's essential passivity regarding sex receives full treatment much earlier in *Cancer.* He is with Van Norden, an agreeably unsavory character who functions as a kind of alter ego, and who, in contrast with Miller, literally does think and talk of nothing but sex. Bessie, the only woman he cannot take to bed, correctly characterizes him as "just a worn-out satyr" who does not "know the meaning of passion" (p. 135). With Miller in tow,

---

24. Jack Mabley, quoted in " 'Cancer' in Chicago," p. 9.

he engages for both of them the invariable nameless and hungry prostitute. The three of them, all equally passionless, retire to Van Norden's room, where Miller's passivity casts him into the role of *voyeur*. "As I watch Van Norden tackle her," he writes,

> it seems to me that I am looking at a machine whose cogs have slipped. . . . I am sitting on a chair behind him, watching their movements with a cool, scientific detachment. . . . It's like watching one of those crazy machines which throw the newspaper out. . . . The machine seems more sensible, crazy as it is, and more fascinating to watch, than the human beings and the events which produced it. My interest in Van Norden and the girl is nil. . . . As long as that spark of passion is missing there is no human significance in the performance. The machine is better to watch. (143)

Here, undoubtedly, is the crux of Miller's problem, for his sexual passivity and general malaise result from that absent spark of passion. In general, as we have seen, he attempts to make the sterility of the world about him into the villain of the piece— even to the point of faulting Paris, the one place where life has been possible for him. At times, however, Miller will attempt a more specific self-analysis, a more intimate delving after the roots of the cancerous growths within him. Of a much earlier period he writes: "things were wrong usually only when one cared too much. That impressed itself on me very early in life. . . . This caring too much—I remember that it only developed with me about the time I first fell in love. And even then I didn't care enough. If I had really cared I wouldn't be here now writing about it. . . . It was a bad experience because it taught me how to live a lie" (Capricorn, 14-15).

The Miller of the *Tropics*, then, is a man who has trained himself to care for no one—and rather than run the risks of emotional involvement attendant upon normal intercourse, he reduces all such contact to the simply sexual. Concomitantly, when

every woman becomes a whore and every whore a single anatomi-
cal feature, the process, as Miller has suggested, is a lie, or rather,
the poetic technique of synecdoche. Like food, then, the simple
animalistic response to sexual stimulus serves as a safe standard,
for it actually involves only a minute fraction of the real personality buried beneath the brutish exterior.

But the buffoon-lecher mask slips occasionally, revealing a
Miller who cares very much indeed. For throughout the autobiographical fiction, as Kingsley Widmer has indicated, there runs
the pivotal theme of

> the misery and inspiration connected with the Dark Lady
> of passion. She is partly the "femme fatale" of the ro-
> mantic, and inverted traditional muse of the artist, the
> Eve-Lilith of primordial knowledge, a witch-goddess of
> sexuality and power, and, according to Miller's insistence,
> his second wife. Under the names of Mona and Mara, she
> haunts most of Miller's work; and she appears, at least
> briefly, in almost every book he has written.[25]

Certainly her appearances are brief and intermittent, for
her story is as fragmented as everything else in Miller's discon-
tinuous narrative. Nonetheless, Miller's treatment of her constantly emphasizes her emotional centrality to his life and to his
work. For one thing, the Mona/Mara passages are remarkably
free of both censorable language and excremental references.
Descriptions of Mona and of scenes with her, unlike those of other
women in the *Tropics,* never become flights of nihilistic, semiab-
stract imagery indulged in for their own sake. Of the significance
of Mona, the "Her" to whom *Capricorn* is dedicated, Miller
writes: "Everything I endured was in the nature of a preparation
for that moment when, putting on my hat one evening, I walked
out of the office, out of my hitherto private life, and sought the
woman who was to liberate me from a living death" (64).

---

25. Widmer, *Henry Miller,* p. 69.

In *Cancer* she appears initially as a figure of almost virginal purity, a kind of antiwhore who embodies love rather than sex. Miller has been eagerly awaiting her return to Paris when "suddenly," he writes,

> I see a pale heavy face with burning eyes—and the little velvet suit that I always adored because under the soft velvet there were always her warm breasts, the marble legs, cool, firm, muscular. She rises up out of a sea of faces and embraces me, embraces me passionately. . . . I sit down beside her and she talks—a flood of talk. . . . I hear not a word because she is beautiful and I love her and now I am happy and willing to die. (27)

Then in bed their intense passion finds expression, as do Miller's tenderness and love—and a new emotion, fear.

> She lies down on the bed with her clothes on. Once, twice, three times, four times . . . I'm afraid she'll go mad . . . in bed, under the blankets, how good to feel her body again! But for how long? Will it last this time? Already I have a presentiment that it won't. . . . Finally she drops off and I pull my arm from under her. My eyes close. Her body is there beside me . . . it will be there till morning surely. . . . My eyes are closed. We breathe warmly into each other's mouth. Close together, America three thousand miles away. I never want to see it again. To have her here in bed with me, breathing on me, her hair in my mouth— I count that something of a miracle. Nothing can happen now till morning." (28)

But in the morning everything happens. They wake to find each other crawling with bedbugs; Mona, needing a bath, food, and adequate clothing, loses her temper at Miller's having for-

gotten to provide for money; and, although Miller does not detail
the rest of the sequence of events, by the next page Mona disap-
pears from the narrative—not to be even mentioned again for
some 120 pages. Again he longs for her, wondering how different
life might be with "a young, restless creature by (his) side"; but
his image of her has altered drastically and, bitterly, he sees her as
alien to his European world. If she ever should return, he wryly
speculates,

> she'll probably tell me right away that it's unsanitary.
> That's the first thing that strikes an American woman
> about Europe—that it's unsanitary. Impossible for them to
> conceive of a Paradise without modern plumbing. . . .
> She'll say I've become a degenerate. I know her line from
> beginning to end. She'll want to look for a studio with a
> garden attached—and a bath-tub to be sure. She wants to
> be poor in a romantic way. I know her. But I'm prepared
> for her this time. (151)

Exactly what is good about being poor in an unromantic
way Miller never explains, but certainly he is correct about being
prepared for her—for he manages, at least for the moment, to blot
from his mind everything that belongs to the past, especially
those few years when they were together and life was, if not edenic,
at least vital and intense. Now when he thinks of her—and he is
not able to keep himself from doing so entirely—it is "not as of a
person in a definite aura of time and space, but separate, detached,
as though she had blown up into a great cloud-like form that
blotted out the past." Regardless, he adds,

> I couldn't allow myself to think about her very long; if I
> had I would have jumped off the bridge. It's strange. I had
> become so reconciled to this life without her; and yet if
> I thought about her only for a minute it was enough to
> pierce the bone and marrow of my contentment and shove

me back again into the agonizing gutter of my wretched
past. (175)

And yet, no matter what the reason, a man who wilfully destroys his past, as Miller begins to realize, commits spiritual suicide: "It seems as if my own proper existence had come to an end
somewhere, just where exactly I can't make out. I'm not an
American any more, nor a New Yorker, and even less a European,
or a Parisian. I haven't any allegiance, any responsibilities, any
hatreds, any worries, any prejudices, any passion. I'm neither for
nor against. I'm a neutral" (*Cancer*, p. 151). But this statement
serves first as manifesto and only subsequently as actual fact, for
after the climactic moment when he recognizes the irrevocable loss
of Mona, he gives way to a despairing loneliness so profound and
so terrible that all else seems irrelevant. Yet in his hopelessness
he comes full cycle, rediscovering his affinity with all the sordid
and cancerous aspects of Paris, a city that "attracts the tortured,
the hallucinated, the great maniacs of love," a Paris that "is like
a whore. From a distance she seems ravishing, you can't wait until
you have her in your arms. And five minutes later you feel empty,
disgusted with yourself. You feel tricked" (178, 204). Ultimately,
there are only the streets for refuge, for the streets take every
man's torments, every man's raging despair that is so precious
because it confirms his significance as an individual capable of
suffering, and the streets make something of it neither for nor
against, but simply neutral. Miller, as we see him last, is a
vastly diminished figure wondering "in a vague way what had
ever happened to (his) wife" (305). "A vague way"—the phrase
is significant—for it suggests, and this is borne out in the later
writings, that the failure of the relationship may well have resulted
from Miller's intrinsic inadequacies. As Widmer has put it: "While
his version of the Dark Lady myth aims to show Miller as the
victim of love, he really presents himself as the victim of his own
lovelessness." [26]
Thus Miller's passionless passivity, his apathetic indifference

26. *Ibid.*, p. 75.

to the things that most of us value in life. He begins his *Tropics* triad as a rebel without a cause—as "a James Dean character, a Hemingway of undisciplined creative yearnings" [27]—and even though he is often ludicrous and ineffectual we are sympathetic, for he is saying things that need to be said; we have heard them before, but they bear the repeating. For, as Miller puts it in *Capricorn*, "even if everything I say is wrong, is prejudiced, spiteful, malevolent, even if I am a liar and a poisoner, it is nonetheless the truth and it will have to be swallowed" (13).

Before very long, however, he is worn out and used up, a causeless nonconformist maintaining the old postures merely because they have become habitual. By the end of *Cancer*, Miller has even run out of defiant gestures. He is sitting in a cafe, idly watching the Seine; his pockets bulging with money—the filthy stuff he has always claimed to depise—money, moreover, he has stolen from a friend. And, perhaps strangest and unkindest cut of all, he speaks the tired conservatism of the *nouveau riche:* ". . . you can't create a revolution," he writes. "You can't wash all the dirt out of your belly" (*Cancer*, p. 304). Thus in *Capricorn* Miller has nowhere to go. "To want to change the condition of affairs," he writes at the beginning of that book, "seemed futile to me; nothing would be altered, I was convinced, except by a change of heart, and who could change the hearts of men?" (9). Miller had thought that he could, but he was wrong. "For a man of my temperament," he adds later in the same book, "the world being what it is, there is absolutely no hope, no solution" (102).

Miller claims that the *Tropics* are about regeneration—"the Dionysian theme which . . . must be the theme for the writers to come—the only theme permissible, or possible." [28] Miller does occasionally employ redemptive imagery—for example, the quietly flowing Seine at the end of *Cancer*—but he seems ultimately incapable of rising from negation to affirmation, incapable of transcending his long dark night of the soul (the very word

---

27. Gertz, *Critics*, p. 177.
28. Henry Miller, in Durrell and Miller, *Correspondence*, p. 78. Miller is speaking specifically of Lawrence Durrell's *The Black Book*, but, by implication, about his own books as well.

"soul", in fact, he finds ludicrous). In *Capricorn* he writes that "whoever, through too great love, which is monstrous after all, dies of his misery, is born again to know neither love nor hate, but to enjoy. And this joy of living, because it is unnaturally acquired, is a poison which eventually vitiates the whole world" (67-68). The *Tropics*, then, is not about redemption at all, but only about the death of love—and the irrevocable finality and waste of one man's spiritual suicide.

Certainly only the naive would attempt to deny that love has indeed pitched its mansion in the place of excrement, but only those uncompromisingly bitter and self-defeating—and Miller is both in these books—attempt to exalt an excremental or merely animalistic standard over that of love. Miller, it seems, would have the cancerous growths of his *Tropics* block out the light entering love's mansion, just as his own memory conveniently blotted out more and more of his painful past. But fortunately, and perhaps despite his intentions, Miller demonstrates that such a perverse disordering is invariably doomed to failure—and this demonstration may well be the one permanent edifice in the jungles of Henry Miller's *Tropics*.

ARTISTS AND ARTISTS:
THE 'AESTHETICS' OF HENRY MILLER

Edward B. Mitchell

It is a commonplace of literary criticism that Plato felt it incumbent to cast the artist out of the Republic because the artist created imitations of imitations, because his work, thrice removed from reality, could not conceivably lead to knowledge of the eternal forms. What is less frequently noticed, however, is that this argument forms only half of Plato's objection to artists and to poetry, and in many respects not the most important half. As Plato goes on to explain to Glaucon, the poets, especially the dramatic poets, are dangerous to the Republic because they appeal to the emotions and the passions, and thus, as Plato puts it in the Conford translation, "one who lends an ear to it [poetry] should rather beware of endangering the order established in his soul. . . ." [1] The artist must be expelled from the Republic because he destroys the carefully erected Platonic psychology wherein the reason, in league with the spirited element of the soul, controls the emotions. The banishment of the artist is the price of the Republic because the artist overturns the psychology of which the Republic itself is only an analogy "writ large."

---

1. F. M. Cornford, trans., *The Republic of Plato* (Oxford, 1957), p. 340.

It is interesting to place Henry Miller in this particular context because unlikely as it might appear, Plato's and Miller's views of the nature of the poet, and his role vis à vis society, are almost identical. The only difference between them is that Miller argues against the banishment of the artist. While Plato argues for rule by philosophers, Miller insists on rule by artists, for it is his conviction that "the true leaders of the world are the men of imagination, the seers. To unite man with man and peoples with peoples is not the work of politicians or of social reformers; men are united only through illumination. The true poet is an awakener; he does not promise bread and jobs. . . . All ideas of government fail insofar as they exclude the poet and the seer who are one." [2] Whereas Plato would expel the artist from the Republic because he appeals to the irrational and imaginative faculties in man, Miller would call back the artist precisely because that is his function, and because, in Miller's view, no republic can operate in any meaningful way without him.

In order to understand why Miller does not share the Platonic conclusion regarding the necessary destiny of the artist, we will need to give some detailed attention to the notion of "the poet and the seer who are one." In so doing, however, it will be well to bear in mind that while Miller has written at some length on major literary figures, including Lawrence, Rimbaud, Proust, Joyce, Balzac, and Whitman, not to mention a considerable list of lesser-known figures, his criticism usually reveals more of his own position than that of the artist being examined. As Miller puts it, "no matter how much I dwell on the works of others I come back inevitably to the one and only book, the book of myself." [3]

Thus, when, in *The Cosmological Eye,* Miller turns his attention to Proust and Joyce, he finds both of them wanting, which is not to say that they fail in what they set out to do, but that their work manifests an orientation sharply different from his own. It is that difference which is instructive. In Proust Miller finds "the full flower of psychologism—confession, self-analysis,

---

2. Henry Miller, *Sunday after the War* (Norfolk, Connecticut, 1961), p. 59.

3. Miller, *The Books in My Life* (Norfolk, Connecticut, 1952), p. 98.

arrest of living, making of art the final justification, but thereby divorcing art from life. An intestinal conflict in which the artist is immolated. . . . A worship of art for its own sake—not for man. Art, in other words, regarded as a means of salvation, as a redemption from suffering, as a compensation for the terror of living. Art as a substitute for life." [4] As Miller sees it, Proust, who thought himself to be making a book of his life, actually succeeded in revealing the plight of the modern man for whom there is no faith, no meaning, no life. Through his microscopic reflections and analysis, Proust immures himself in his art, for him "life was not a living, but a feasting upon sunken treasures, a life of retrospect." [5] In the work of Joyce, Miller finds the process of "soul deterioration" carried to even greater lengths, for "if Proust may be said to have provided the tomb of art, in Joyce we can witness the full process of decomposition." [6] *Ulysses,* is a paean to the atomization of man. In Miller's opinion, both Proust and Joyce are offering a picture of the world-as-disease, but Joyce's work is even more of a tomb than Proust's, because "through his chaos and obscenity, his obsessions and complexes, his perpetual, frantic search for God, Joyce reveals the desperate plight of the modern man who, lashing about in his steel and concrete cage, admits finally that there is no way out." [7]

The focal point for the preceding is actually a three-way comparison of Lawrence, Proust, and Joyce which was to form part of a projected, but never completed, book on Lawrence, of whom Miller says:

> Despite all that may be said against him, as an or as a man, he still remains the most alive, the most vitalizing of recent

4. Miller, *The Cosmological Eye* (Norfolk, Connecticut, 1961), pp. 109-110. This is the American reprint of the earlier *Max and the White Phagocytes* excluding the essay "The Eye of Paris," and including from *Black Spring,* "Jabberwhorl Cronstadt," "Into the Night Life," "The Tailor Shop," and three other essays: "Peace," "It's Wonderful," "The Brooklyn Bridge," and "Autobiographical Note."

5. Miller, *The Cosmological Eye,* p. 126.

6. *Ibid.,* p. 110.

7. *Ibid.,* p. 111.

writers. Proust had to die in order even to commence his great work; Joyce, though still alive, seems even more dead than Proust ever was. Lawrence on the other hand, is still with us: his death, in fact, is a mockery of the living. Lawrence killed himself in the effort to burst the bonds of living death. There is no evidence for believing, if we study for example such a work as The Man Who Died, that had it been given him to enjoy the normal span of life he would have arrived at a state of wisdom, a mystic way of life, in which the artist and the human being would have been reconciled.[8]

Here we find, in contradiction to "living death," that "mystic way of life" which is Miller's doctrine of acceptance under another name, this time found manifest in, or perhaps projected upon, the figure of Lawrence. And although, in Miller's opinion, Lawrence never successfully effected the reconciliation between the artist and the human being, still "it is against the stagnant flux in which we are now drifting that Lawrence appears brilliantly alive. Proust and Joyce needless to say, appear more representative: they 'reflect' the times. We see in them no revolt: it is surrender, suicide, and the more poignant since it springs from creative sources." [9] In short, the difference Miller finds between Lawrence, on the one hand, and Proust and Joyce, on the other, is a qualitive difference, whereas the difference between Joyce and Proust is largely one of degree. In Miller's view, Lawrence was struggling to reassert the aristocracy of the individual, and to relate the individual to the cosmic processes surrounding and sustaining him. Lawrence's work, although not completely realized, was a hymn of affirmation, whereas in Proust and Joyce, Miller finds the keening accompanying a burial. Proust, defeated by reality, withdraws and makes of art a substitute for life, he lives only in the remembrance of things past. Joyce, for his part, hurls himself into

---

8. *Ibid.*, p. 108.
9. *Ibid.*, p. 109.

the abyss of the night mind and through a chronicle of dirty Dublin reveals the defeat of man in a war of attrition.

Whatever the excesses of such an interpretation, Miller's central point is still discernible. Although he finds much of the "poet" in Proust and Joyce, he finds none of the "seer." For Miller, the only adequate definition of the artist is "the poet and the seer who are one." But such a definition clearly implies that Miller holds an unusual view both of what art is and what it does. One conviction, which he repeats throughout his work, is particularly relevant here. He repeatedly insists that art, as that term is generally understood, must be transcended: "I believe that one has to pass beyond the sphere and influence of art. Art is only a means to life, the life more abundant. It is not in itself the life more abundant. It merely points the way, something which is overlooked not only by the public, but very often by the artist himself. In becoming an end it defeats itself." [10] In Miller's view there are two possible defeats involved here. First, the artist himself may be defeated if he makes his art a substitute for life, if he becomes totally immured in his own realm of symbol and fantasy. Secondly, the purpose of art is defeated if the audience accepts any work of art as a fulfillment, as a final statement, rather than as an appeal to a greater liberation of the imaginative faculties, a fuller, richer, more meaningful means of viewing the world. And both of these are related in that art, in two different ways, has become an end in itself.

Proust and Joyce, then, have permitted art to become an end in itself. However, Miller insists that not only is this unnecessary, it is in fact the mark of those who are not truly artists. The true artist, the poet-seer, is one who views art as a means for attaining a particular end:

> Strange as it may seem today to say, the aim of life is to
> live, and to live means to be aware, joyously, drunkenly,

---

10. Miller, *The Wisdom of the Heart* (Norfolk, Connecticut, 1960), p. 24.

serenely, divinely aware. In this state of god-like awareness one sings; in this realm the world exists as a poem. . . .
This is the sublime, the a-moral state of the artist, he who
lives only in the moment, the visionary moment of utter,
far-seeing lucidity. Such clear, icy sanity that it seems like
madness. By the force and power of the artist's vision
the static, synthetic whole which is called the world is
destroyed. The artist gives back to us a vital, singing
universe, alive in all its parts.[11]

Miller goes on to assert that "when he the poet-seer succeeds in
establishing this criterion of passionate experience . . . then, and
only then, is he asserting his humanness. Then only does he live
out his pattern as Man." [12] Rather obviously, Miller's definition
of the artist is basically charismatic; and we find here also his
characteristic insistence that being "aware" is the criterion for
being human. Furthermore, he asserts that "the artist's dream of
the impossible, the miraculous, is simply the resultant of his
inability to adapt himself to reality." [13] We need to be aware,
however, that the "reality" Miller means here is what he considers
the insane reality of the unartistic everyday world, the miscon-
ception of reality that is "the static, synthetic whole which is
called the world." In other words, we have here a statement very
much like Blake's when he said that he did not see the sun,
but rather a bright golden guinea. This part of Miller's view,
then, is semiorthodox: the poet-seer lives out his humanness only
when he images forth his experience of reality which is his vision.
  But some of Miller's statements on the artist-art relationship
are highly unorthodox. On the one hand they amount to an
oblique reference to what the seer sees; on the other hand they
entail an examination of the kind of art produced by those who
are not seers. At one point, Miller elaborates an expanded image
of what he calls the tree of life and death, which he sees as a

----

11. *Ibid.,* pp. 2-3.
12. *Ibid.,* p. 3.
13. *Ibid.,* p. 4.

combined artistic-historical metaphor. Employing the terms of the metaphor, Miller asserts that the creative individual gives ever greater expression to his life instincts until at the last limits of creativeness he is suddenly faced with the incontestable fact of his human limitations, his human finitude. The tree of life now becomes the tree of death. The creative individual now returns to the roots of his being and finds that rather than attempt to transcend death he must accept and incorporate it. In the process of facing this mystery of life and death, the individual is awakened to a totality larger than himself—he perceives the underlying unity of life. As Miller puts it:

> It is this acceptance of the laws of one's being which preserves the vital instincts of life, even in death. In the rush upward the "individual" aspect of one's being was the imperative, the only obsession. But at the summit, when the limits have been felt and perceived, there unfolds the grand perspective and one recognizes the similitude of surrounding beings, the interrelationship of all forms and laws of being—the "organic" relatedness, the wholeness, the oneness of life.[14]

What the artist as achetype becomes is a seer. And if we work through the enigmatic metaphor Miller chooses as his vehicle of expression, we find that what the seer sees is a vision very much like Miller's own, for the creative individual accepts the laws of being with his realization of the "organic relatedness, the wholeness, the oneness of life."

In Miller's view, the true artist comes to accept and convert his human limitations because the struggle between his creative instincts and his eventual death, the starkest reminder of his human finitude, catapults him into an intuitive awareness of a transcendent and overriding unity. Paradoxically, the acceptance of death frees him to live. To attempt to glean any more meaning

---

14. *Ibid.*, p. 10.

from Miller's metaphor in context is perhaps impossible; but more importantly, it is unnecessary. Miller is less interested in what the artist-seer sees than in the fact that he "does" see, because, as we shall note shortly, Miller insists that the artist-seer's vision is necessarily never wholly translatable. What Miller turns to instead is a consideration of the kind of art produced by those who are not seers. Here he finds that what such art reflects finally is the frustration of the would-be artist who can neither deny nor accept his human finitude: ". . . by living into his art he adopts for his world an intermediary realm in which he is all-powerful, a world which he dominates and rules. This intermediary realm of art, this world in which he moves as hero, was made realizable only out of the deepest sense of frustration." [15] Unaware of the transcendent unity and ultimate purposefulness which pervades the shifting temporality, but spurred by his creative impulses, the artist retreats into his art; and Miller concludes that "his whole art is the pathetic and heroic effort to deny his human defeat. He works out, in his art, an unreal triumph—since it is neither a triumph over life nor over death. It is a triumph over an imaginary world which he himself created." [16] In short, Miller is convinced that in the type of art which forms his standard of judgment, which is to say the art of the seer, there is an element of truth not to be found on any other level than the level of vision. The world reflected in the art of the seers is not "an imaginary world he has created," but the world of reality to which he has awakened.

However, when Miller has separated the sheep from the goats on this fundamental level, when he finds that "vision" is the standard of judgment for art, as "seer" is the quality which forms the standard of judgment for the artist, he is still faced with the fact that for the artist "qua" artist, whether seer or not, there is a sense in which he must "live into his art." The artist must, by the very nature of his creative act, turn upon himself; he must draw upon his own memory, thought, experience, he must withdraw from life and project himself into the work growing under

---

15. *Ibid.,* p. 7.
16. *Ibid.*

his hands. Miller concedes this necessity and phrases it this way: "In order to accomplish his purpose, however, the artist is obliged to retire, to withdraw from life, utilizing just enough of experience to present the flavor of the real struggle. If he chooses to 'live' he defeats his own nature. He 'must' live vicariously." [17] Here, it would appear, Miller has involved himself in a fundamental contradiction. If the artist chooses simply to live, rather than create, he denies his nature as artist. On the other hand, so long as he creates works of art, he withdraws from life, he does not live according to the dictates of his awareness, rather he lives vicariously. Yet it is exactly vicarious living which is anathema to Miller.

Yet this difficulty, encountered by the artist-seer in relation to his art, forms only one half of the problem. From Miller's point of view the relationship of the audience to art can entail a danger of equal magnitude. In the attempts to come to grips with the vision of the seer imaged in the work of art, the audience may take the work as a fulfillment, a final statement, thus making of the artist's effort a lie which enchants and enslaves rather than an intimation which incites and liberates. Miller is speaking to this point when he says:

> Unconsciously I think that every great artist is trying with might and main to destroy art. By that I mean that he is desperately striving to break down this wall between himself and the rest of humanity. Not for the sake of the brotherhood of man . . . but in the hope of debouching into some more quick and vivid realm of human experience. He is not struggling to isolate himself from his fellow-men, since it is his very isolation which drives him to create, but rather to emancipate himself from false relations with his fellow-men, from false relations with nature and with all the objects which surround him. Art is only one of the manifestations of the creative spirit. What every great artist is manifesting in his work is a desire to lead

17. *Ibid.*, p. 8.

a richer life, his work itself is only a description, an intimation, as it were, of those possibilities. The worst sin that
can be committed against the artist is to take him at his
word, to see in his work a fulfillment instead of an
horizon.[18]

If what the work of all great artists manifests is a desire to "lead
a richer life," then by implication what such artists desire for their
audience is that they may go and do likewise. Miller states as
much when he says that "what he [the artist-seer] clamors for,
avowedly or unavowedly, is a new deal—in other words, freedom.
His idea of freedom is life lived imaginatively." [19] Thus the
greatest sin that could be committed against the artist is to take
him "at his word," to find in his work a final answer, a fulfillment,
a plan to be adopted, rather than an intimation of possibility. Art,
in Miller's opinion, should serve to awaken the audience, it should
instill in the perceiver a sense that at bottom art is aimed at
"Making poetry, or if you will, of making life a poem. It has
to do with the adoption of a creative attitude toward life." [20]

  The question remains, however, if the audience is to take a
creative attitude toward life, what is it that the audience is to
create? The blunt, and perhaps unsatisfying, answer is that Miller
does not say, or at least he never makes an explicit answer. There
is, however, a reason why Miller does not, indeed cannot, answer
this question, and part of that reason is that he sees the aim of
art as one of abolishing the audience altogether. For Miller, the
intent of all true art is to make artists of the audience. But in
order to understand why and how Miller sees this as coming about,
we shall have to return to the relationship of the artist to his art,
which is finally the cornerstone of Miller's "aesthetics."

  The situation then is this: if the artist does not, in Miller's
case for example, write, then he is denying his nature as artist.

  18. Miller, *The Cosmological Eye,* pp. 167-168.
  19. Miller, *Stand Still Like the Hummingbird* (Norfolk, Connecticut,
1962), p. 60.
  20. Miller, *The Cosmological Eye,* p. 152.

If he does write, he is not living according to his awareness, but he is living vicariously.   In *Sexus* Miller makes the effort to come to terms with this problem; and we might note, parenthetically, that The Rosy Crucifixion is a trilogy which in one sense begins with the question of how and why to write, which in the course of the novels becomes transmuted into the larger question of why and how to become an artist on another level. After once again restating the problem, Miller says:

> No man ever puts down what he intended to say: the original creation, which is taking place all the time, whether one writes or doesn't write, belongs to the primal flux: it has no dimensions, no form, no time element. In this preliminary state, which is creation and not birth, what disappears suffers no destruction; something which was already there, something imperishable, like memory, or matter, or God, is summoned and in it one flings himself like a twig into a torrent. Words, sentences, ideas, no matter how subtle or ingenious, the maddest flights of poetry, the most profound dreams, the most hallucinating visions, are but crude hieroglyphs chiselled in pain and sorrow to commemorate an event which is untransmissible. In an intelligently ordered world there would be no need to make the unreasonable attempt of putting such miraculous happenings down.[21]

The real value of art, for Miller, is the "original creation," and the essential benefit of art therefore is bestowed upon the artist. However, Miller insists that

> It is only in the measure that he [the artist-seer] is aware of more life, the life abundant, that he may be said to live in his work. If there is no realization there is no purpose or

---

21. Miller, *Sexus* (Paris, 1962), p. 27.

advantage in substituting the imaginative life for the purely adventurous one of reality. Every one who lifts himself above the activities of the daily round does so not only in the hope of enlarging his field of experience, or even of enriching it, but of quickening it.[22]

If the artist is not aware, and if he does not see the preliminary act, the creation, before writing, as the real value of art, then, at least as far as Miller is concerned, he is likely to be writing from no better motive than power, fame, success. But when the preliminary act of creation is seen to be the unique value of art, then the artist realizes that "the process in which he is involved has to do with another dimension of life, that by identifying himself with this process he augments life." [23]

The word "augment" is central here. In Miller's view the artist-seer does not alter life, in the sense that one builds a machine, or discovers a drug, or invents a process; rather, he realizes that through his art, at least the preliminary part, he is putting himself in unison with life. And, although no artist can put down exactly what he intended to say, he still augments life both for himself in the period of creation, as well as for others in the imaging forth of his vision which is aimed at enlarging, enriching, and quickening the experience of life. Miller is not so much attempting to escape between the horns of his dilemma as he is attempting to transcend it, for he is convinced that "an author hopes that in giving himself to the world he will enrich and augment life, not deny and denigrate it. If he believed in direct intervention, he would be a healer and not a writer. If he believed that he had the power to eliminate evil and sorrow, he would be a saint, not a spinner of words. Art 'is' a healing process, as Nietzsche pointed out. But mainly for those who practice it." [24] But practice is the important point. If the artist

---

22. *Ibid.*, p. 269.
23. *Ibid.*
24. Miller, *Big Sur and the Oranges of Hieronymus Bosch* (Norfolk, Connecticut, 1957), p. 400.

is aware of "original creation," if he comes to realize the value of the eternal process into which he can fling himself like a twig into a torrent, with or without writing, if he does succeed in penetrating into some more quick and vivid realm of human experience, then he need not fear denying his nature as artist, be he writer, painter, sculptor. In short, a man cannot do nothing. For Miller, it is not a question of whether one is a writer, but whether one is an Artist, and the capital "A" is intentional. For if a man is aware, then he is an Artist; and if he happens also to be an artist, which is to say, in Miller's case, a writer, then he can fulfill his nature as artist because his art will be both an expression of, and his living out, his awareness.

Because the essential value of art, in Miller's opinion, accrues to the artist before words are set to paper, a finished work, a book, an artifact, is limited in its effect upon the audience. As Miller puts it, "a great work of art, if it accomplishes anything, serves to remind us, or let us say to set us to dreaming, of all that is fluid and intangible—which is to say,"the universe." [25] The value of art for the reader or viewer is a by-product of the intrinsic value received by the artist; and thus the extrinsic value of a work of art is the chance of setting more people to dreaming. Still, what the artist-seer really desires is a world in which there would be no necessity for treating in "crude hieroglyphs" events which are not finally and wholly transmissible. The attaining of this condition is, however, an individual process; if art helps to forward this process, it can do so only to the extent that it awakens the audience, that it liberates the imaginative faculties of the audience and makes it aware of its own potential Artistry.

What the artist-seer desires is to emancipate the creative spirit of the audience. It is in this sense that the artist is trying to destroy art, for the essential effect of art is to awaken the audience; the artist's intent is to make Artists, though not necessarily artists, of the audience. Miller denies that he is interested in a cult of artists; rather, he is interested in fostering the faculty of vision in every man because he is certain that art,

---

25. Miller, *Sexus*, p. 27.

when properly understood, is the province of all men. Miller
makes this point when he asserts:

> . . . art is only a stepping-stone to reality; it is the vestibule
> in which we undergo the rites of initiation. Man's task is
> to make himself a work of art. The creations which man
> makes manifest have no validity in themselves; they serve
> to awaken, that is all. And that, of course, is a great deal.
> But it is not the all. Once awakened, everything will
> reveal itself to man as creation. Once the blinders have
> been removed and the fetters unshackled, man will have
> no need to recreate through the elect cult of genius.
> Genius will be the norm.[26]

"Genius is the norm" once man becomes aware; and we might
note that this phrase becomes Miller's variation on Wordsworth's
definition of the poet. We recall that Wordsworth describes the
poet as a man like other men, only possessing a more lively sensibility, more enthusiasm, more tenderness—one who differs from
his fellow men in degree, not in kind. While Wordsworth maintains that the poet is like other men, Miller insists that other men
are like his conception of the poet; and if art has any purpose,
it is to make the audience aware of that underlying similarity; if
it has any power, it is the power to awaken the perceiver, to
break down the "false relations" which exist between the artist
and his fellow man.

We might note also that Miller's comments are not drawn
entirely from, nor applied exclusively to, the realm of art "qua"
art. At least once, in an essay titled "Artist and Public," Miller has
taken up the question of the role of art on a more "practical"
level. After discussing a plan for the maintenance of struggling
artists, and while elaborating on a means for bringing contemporary art to the attention of all, Miller notes that "what is
demanded of a society, what gives it life, is the ability to inspire

---

26. Miller, *Sunday After the War,* pp. 155-156.

a greater measure of enthusiasm, a greater measure of freedom." [27]
A Utopia, even of art, is a dream, and dreams invariably outstrip
accomplished actuality, which is what makes the imaginative
dream of the artist-seer the "sine qua non" of a creative society.
The important point for Miller is that "people have to be
encouraged to make things themselves, in their own fashion,
according to their own limited aesthetic instincts." [28] In this sense
the comparative degree is essential to Miller's point of view—the
measure of the artist-seer's achievement is itself measurable in
terms of a greater enthusiasm and a greater freedom. The role
of art is one of inspiring not awe or appreciation, but creativity:
"the only tenable attitude towards art is to foster the artist in every
human being, see to it that everything one handles, sees or hears
is imbued with art." [29]

Obviously, this is neither balanced social philosophy nor
unbiased literary criticism. Indeed, the point is that it is not.
As we noted earlier, Miller's treatment of other artists tends to
reveal much more about Miller than about the artist under
discussion. For Miller, the experience of awakening is central and
the chief characteristic of that experience is an intuitive insight
into an inclusive, transcendent unity which resolves contradictions; and the experience of that insight, that awakening, comes
with an emotional intensity producing a complete certainty of
conviction. Thus the experience upon which the "aesthetics" is
based goes far to explain the exhortative cast of the prose. Moreover, the seer who is also a writer must employ language, but
language is by and large what Miller has called a "grammar
of thought," [30] and since what the artist-seer has to communicate
is not thought, which is to say that his vision is not logical, inferen-
tial, and discursive, he is driven to paradox or symbology or both.

Thus, on the one hand, Miller appears to be using reason
against rationalism: the value of irrationlism is presented in a

---

27. Miller, *Remember to Remember* (Norfolk, Connecticut, 1960),
p. 414.

28. *Ibid.,* p. 413.

29. *Ibid.,* p. 415.

30. Miller, *The Wisdom of the Heart,* p. 4.

semirational manner. On the other hand, he tends to see relationships and to use terms anagogically. The creativity of the artist is an anagoge to that large creativity, which we might call a mode of reality as process. Furthermore, the anagogic use of terms and relationships has a double effect. First, once Miller establishes certain terms, for example creativity, artist awakening, acceptance, for use in this way, he tends to reiterate them and the repetition adds to the reader's sense of exhortation. Secondly, the exhortation is annoyingly unprogrammatic, the anagoges appear to lead nowhere. Just as one cannot prescribe what form the creativity of the artist shall take, so one cannot prescribe what form the creativity of the seer shall take. Or to put it another way, what one does is dependent upon what one is, and what one is is dependent upon one's awareness or the lack of it, and for the acquisition of awareness there is no program.

What a position such as Miller's amounts to, in effect, is a denial of significant difference on any but the most fundamental level. The word "significant" is important because Miller admits differences and indulges in them to the point of contradiction— he simply denies that such differences are significant. To put it affirmatively, Miller asserts that contraries are not mutually exclusive, but rather aspects of a unity which when perceived resolves contradictions. But the lack of perception, the failure to be aware, is significant; and what this means, on the level of art, is the denial that Proust and Joyce, for example, have a vision. Rather than seeing in the work of Joyce and Proust a manifestation of a vision different from his own, Miller simply sees their art as a manifestation of a lack of vision. The point is, however, that this appears to be the inevitable outcome of the positive advocacy of the notion of awareness. The fact that Miller has in a sense only one string to his critical, as well as aesthetic, lyre is directly traceable to his insistence on the notion of "the poet and the seer who are one." Yet, Miller's aesthetic position does reveal an internal consistency which permits Miller a complicated, if not complex, solution to his artist-seer dilemma, while offering only an irritatingly single-minded criterion for the judgment of art. Furthermore, it is the kind of consistency which allows Miller to find that the social function of the artist is of the highest

importance for the same reason that Plato found it keenly disturbing, while still permitting Miller to insist that the artist-seer has
no program to offer his fellow man.

But in spite of the nonrational, intuitional nature of Miller's
position, in spite of the fact that he insists that "we can never
explain except in terms of new conundrums [because] what
belongs to realm of the spirit, or the eternal, evades all explanation," Miller still does not feel that he is unique, that he is
isolated. On the contrary, it is the very notion of awareness
which establishes for him the real nature of tradition because

> . . . it reveals the genuine role of the poet and the true
> nature of tradition. Of what use the poet unless he attains
> to a new vision of life, unless he is willing to sacrifice his
> life in attesting the truth and the splendor of his vision?
> It is the fashion to speak of these demonic beings, these
> visionaries, as Romantics, to stress their subjectivity and to
> regard them as breaks, interruptions, stopgaps in the great
> stream of tradition, as though they were madmen whirling
> about the pivot of self. Nothing could be more untrue.
> It is precisely these innovators who form the links in the
> great chain of creative literature. One must indeed begin
> at the horizons where they expire—"hold the gain," as
> Rimbaud puts it—and not sit down comfortably in the
> ruins and piece together a puzzle of shards.[31]

In the ranks of these visionaries Miller places, again at the expense
of differences, such figures as Gerald de Nerval, Dostoyevsky,
Whitman, Strindberg, Nietzsche, Baudelaire, Hamsun, Rimbaud,
Blake, and Lautreamont, among others.[32] What Miller finds these
figures to have in common is that, rather than shore fragments
against their ruins, they have attained to a new vision of life.

---

31. Miller, *The Time of the Assassins* (Norfolk, Connecticut, 1946),
p. 87.
32. See the "coda" to *Time of the Assassins*, pp. 159-163.

For all their differences, they manifest the underlying and unifying quality of the "seer." And even more importantly, Miller finds that these visionaries are united in the common cause of making themselves unnecessary. Their interest is to liberate the creative spirit, to bequeath the power of vision; and to Miller's lights this is a continuous possibility because a vision is realized the moment one begins to live by it.

THE ART OF MILLER:
THE MIND AND ART OF HENRY MILLER

William Gordon

Henry Miller's cycle of autobiographical novels develops on the same principle as the diaries of Anaïs Nin. In the original plan one large work would incorporate the material from the central period of his life, from his first marriage to his flight to Paris. The original plan expanded to include four works, *Tropic of Capricorn* and the three books of *The Rosy Crucifixion.* Obviously the plan could not have been complete at the time he made it in 1927 because he had not yet become a writer, and that destiny had to be present in order to give direction to the development. By the time he actually wrote *Tropic of Capricorn* in the late thirties, he had already published *Tropic of Cancer* and *Black Spring,* among other shorter pieces, and his career as a writer was sufficiently established to make it the goal of his development in the auto-novels.

The key to autobiographical form is the search for individual identity; and in his use of that form, Miller resembles in many ways, so far little noted, the great nineteenth-century Romantics. Even among the English Romantics the search for individual identity took the form of a descent into the lower levels of psychic life, a passing out of the self in order to discover the relation of the individual to the cosmos and the interaction of art with life. The form is most apparent, however, in those writers who chose autobiography as their typical mode of expression—Wordsworth in England and Thoreau, Emerson, and Whitman in America. The autobiographical poem as it appears in Wordsworth and Whitman is radically different from the personal lyric in that it tries to render an experience going on in time; its inner principle is the ideal of growth.

The idea of self-creation which appears most fully in the poetry of Wordsworth and Whitman presupposes a philosophy of nature which makes ultimate harmony possible. This philosophy has to be antimechanistic because it has to abolish the split between matter and spirit. The romantic philosophy of nature envisioned man as having his roots deep in nature, a nature which was not excluded from man. Thus man on the deepest levels of his being participated in nature, and upon this participation depended his sense of joy. Ultimately the romantic philosophy had to be individualistic because the experience of unity could not be taught; it was a journey which each man had to make for himself. Though the Romantics were attracted by the idea of creating a new philosophy of life, they were necessarily unsuccessful. They could only offer the example, which other men might imitate, of the successful growth of one individual.

Once the idea of self-creation had been grasped, there followed the notion that each man might be an artist with respect to his own life, whether he produced artistic works or not. Such a close relation of art and life led to the paradox that a poem ostensibly about life could be read as a poem about the artist and his art, and that its theme could be understood as having pertinence to the life of every man. The experience of the artist became the prototype for the experience of man creating himself. Thus the artist could use as the material of his art the creative process itself, and the creative process thus rendered would have relevance to the life of every man.

The romantic insight into the close relation of man to nature and the relevance of the creative process to the life of every individual failed to affect the development toward the industrialized collective society which we now see full blown. It may well be that the full significance of the romantic revolt had to wait until the developments in philosophy, psychology, and sociology had borne out the original insights of the great Romantics. Because those insights have now been made explicit, they have furnished the basis for a resurgence of these attitudes. In some ways, of course, romanticism has never died, and the individualism of the modern artist in his opposition to the regimentation of society is an expression of that romanticism. But revolt alone does not make the romantic. It is necessary that there be some destiny toward which the individual is developing, some vision to be expressed in life and art.

The nineteenth-century Romantics did not achieve any real solution to the historic conflicts within the data of consciousness. As awareness expanded, these conflicts could not be reconciled with the system of moral, political, and social absolutes. Wordsworth, who extolled the common life, gave no hint of vulgarity among the vulgar. Even his own erotic adventures were well covered up. Coleridge went furthest, perhaps, in suggesting the extremes of experience, though on a symbolic level only. The cavernous depths of "Kubla Khan," the "demon lover," the ambiguities of Geraldine, suggest Jungian depths long before Jung. Whitman even more explicitly explored the range of his own feeling and, through sympathy, that of other men. The shocked repudiation of Whitman in his own times testifies to the degree of his success.

Wordsworth still hoped that life and art would intersect, but they could not, even for him. Keats more wisely created a poetic solution. For him death was too obviously the end of life to allow him the illusion of a real unification of all experience, of mortality and immortality, of real and ideal. During the later nineteenth and the early twentieth century, however, a postevolutionary romanticism uncovered new problems and new solutions. The world of moral and philosophical absolutes within which the early Romantics worked was attacked first by Darwin, then by Einstein. From the debris of Western thought arose not one but a variety of ways to deal with the new situation. Idealism, pragmatism, scientism, instrumentalism, in addition to what was left over from the previous age provided more of a market place for ideas than a coherent system of thought. With the decline in external guides, we find a growth in subjectivism. Man turns, in the absence of alternatives, to the data of his own consciousness of reality for help and direction.[1] Philosophical, psychological, and artistic developments helped support and advance this new direction. The men who led the scientific and artistic revolt . . . are the new romantics. The new vision of life to be achieved by art and by thought were no longer separated by the irreconcilable opposites of traditional Western moral, theological, and philosophical absolutes. With the shift in point of view from self and the world to world in the self—that is to self-awareness as primary—the way was open, theoretically at least, to unify even life and death. If eternity could be conceived as the moment expanded into eternity, then even death was illusory. Eternity ceased to be something which followed life; it existed as an ever-present possibility, here and now. The divsion of time horizontally into past and present was to be replaced by the vertical line of human awareness. Through increasing awareness the illusion of past and present would finally disappear. To integrate that view into the experience of life was the task of the artist. Henceforth joy was to be unmixed with melancholy.[2]

It has been my purpose to show that Henry Miller belongs to this new romantic tradition, and that his art is characterized by a different concept of the role of the artist than that which formal criticism has elaborated since World War I. Philip Rahv criticized Miller because he could not "afford the continual sacrifice of personality that the act of creation requires.. . . ."[3] But in Miller'ïs world nothing is left except personality, and the artist has no choice but to make his life the material of his

---

1. This, too, finds support in Peckham's theory that in periods of stress when traditional standards of value are lost, man turns to himself for his sole guide.

2. Dostoyevski presented this idea through Kirilov in *The Possessed*. Philosophers, artists, and mystics who turn toward consciousness itself as the ultimate reality discount objective time as illusory. Pure duration can conceivably be extended infinitely. Under certain conditions this view is able to admit a God-force in the world, but refuses to put salvation in any world other than this one.

3. Rahv, *Image and Idea*, 163.

art. We may hold, if we like, that such an art is better or worse than the objective art which Rahv is talking about, but we must at least perform the critical task of showing how such an art is organized and what the nature of its communication is.

The form of Miller's art we shall call autobiographical, for want of a better name. Miller's own term, "auto-novels," performs several valuable functions. It distinguishes between what is fictional or constructive and what is personal and autobiographical. As in the autobiographical form of Wordsworth and Whitman, the events and thoughts of the central character are from experience, for the most part at least; but the structure, which formal critics admit to being an aspect of meaning, is created by the artist. Since the goal of the work is a destiny to be achieved—a point at which art and life intersect and art passes into life—then the structure has a special form which is necessary to attain that end. The best descriptive analogy for that form is taken from music, the art of the figure. Thus, in structure, the art of the autobiographical artist will more closely resemble the fugue than the symphony. The same themes and motifs will be repeated many times, leading not so much to a climax as to an accumulation of meaning which is sensed as more and more significant. Each time a familiar fragment appears it acquires a slightly new meaning by reason of the new context.[4] Romantic autobiography has a tendency to appear repetitive unless we become aware that each reappearance of the familiar theme results in a greater realization by the author of his precise destiny. The overall theme is based on the idea of growth toward fulfillment, of the conversion of vital energy into form, which enhances the individual's sense of identity and completion.

Thus we must search for the form of Henry Miller's work in his total development toward his goals in life, not in each individual work, though these too have their own partial forms. Each single work expresses a fragment of insight, an insight which frequently will concern the frustration of the protagonist who finds himself momentarily without sense of direction. Miller has

---

4. Wallace Fowlie has applied the fugal analogy to the works of Gide in Fowlie, *Clowns and Angels* (New York: Sheed and Ward, 1943), 17.

said that his work is the story of his life, which is very true if we
assume that a significant part of his experience grew out of his
work. Miller's art, as I see it, is devoted to the creation of both
his life and his work, in the sense that he brought together those
elements of his life which showed a continuity of development
toward the goals he wished to achieve. He emphasizes in his development a growth from the frustrated individual caught in a
hostile society to the man who has achieved his life goals, who has
become self-sufficient and independent. To that extent his achievement does not differ greatly from that of Wordsworth and Whitman. Yet Miller is different, and he is different precisely to the
extent that he is doing consciously what the Romantics did by
intuition. Miller, who was as we have seen widely read in romantic
literature, had access to the researches of psychology, through which
he could more consciously give form to the development in depth
of the individual life. At the center of Miller's art is his blending of
conscious and apparently unconscious material. Miller has drawn,
as any writer must, upon unconscious material, but mainly he
has created a myth of the unconscious to carry out his basic
journey theme. The conscious creation of a myth is indicated
by the importance Miller attached to Freud's statement "Into the
night life are relegated the things that belonged to the day."
Presumably, as the myth goes, before the growth of consciousness
and the appearance of civilization, the primary instincts were
closer to the surface, not only available, but continually active
in life. These instincts, being to civilized man less necessary, or at
least inappropriate, sank from sight into the prehuman animal
level which characterizes the unconscious processes. Unhappily,
the frustration that follows from the too frequent and too rigid
denial of these instincts creates serious problems for civilized
man in attaining satisfaction. Thence issue discontent and even
neuroses.

What we must note in connection with Miller is that he not
only refused to renounce the satisfaction of his needs, but that he
used as the material of his art the very needs themselves. The
recovery of the past in his autobiographical romance became the
means of clarifying for himself the full nature of these needs.
This quality of his art has been noted by Lawrence Durell: ". . . he

has retained (as every artist must) an abnormally large part of his childhood fantasy life intact—with all its wounds and ardours and fantastically *unreasonable* demands upon the world, upon men. He has re-enacted it all as an adult, and then written it all out, unwittingly providing a catharsis for the dammed-up phantasy life of the Anglo-Saxon." [5] The past as Miller relived it was a period of almost untrammeled joy, a time when the world was "forever warm and still to be enjoyed." Not only Miller, but his friends as well were always open to experience. The demands made by the world destroyed his friends. Miller, feeling the same demands upon himself, reacted with the full force of his own destructive energy. The manner of Miller's acting during the period of his young manhood until he met Mona is a revelation of the full scope of man's capacity to unleash his own primitive aggressions against the world. There can be little doubt that the levels of life which Miller is expressing here are highly regressive, associated with infantile demands upon reality.

We have dealt previously with the food-sex imagery in *Tropic of Cancer*. Certainly the interchangeability of food and sex indicates an early level of human desire, which reveal at the same time certain tendencies to destructiveness through incorporation. More important to an understanding of the significant sexual passages in *Tropic of Capricorn* and *The Rosy Crucifixion* is an awareness of the manner in which aggression is expressed through the sexual act itself. Whereas Miller's sexual experience with Mona has a certain primitive violence, he has a less destructive attitude to her. The sexual experiences with those women who mean less to him become almost sadistic encounters in which he uses the sexual organ more like a weapon than an instrument of pleasure. He expresses this attitude indirectly in his cultivated detachment from the woman as he brings her to an orgasm and directly, as in this passage with Rita Schnadig, with the words: "I could have held it indefinitely—it was incredible how detached I was and yet thoroughly aware of every quiver and jolt she made. But somebody had to pay for making me walk around in the rain grubbing a dime. Somebody had to pay for the ecstasy

5. Perles and Durrell, *Art and Outrage,* 54.

produced by the germination of all those unwritten books inside me." [6]

If this destructiveness is indeed to be associated with earlier states of human development, the question arises as to whether the author is writing out of the sickness of permanent regression, or whether he is able, as Freud suggested, to regress deliberately to earlier states in order to use the material for his art. We should assume, I believe, that Miller's reactions are within the scope of normality. Faced with a deadening society which wants him to adopt death as life, he is fighting to preserve his openness to experience and to himself. Most men are open in childhood, but in the course of adjusting themselves to society they lose their flexibility, originality, and self-identity. Therefore, at this juncture Miller turns to the period when openness was the habitual condition, when the energy to keep that openness was fully available, that is, childhood. In reorganizing the experience of childhood, he regains at the same time the full intensity of childhood demands, even to the point of awakening the oral demands of infancy and the narcissistic needs of earlier stages of growth. The artist shows his health in being able to submit this material to the demands of literary form, and for Miller this meant assimilating the material from his past life into his autobiographical romance.

Miller's use of fantasy I take to be an artistic and symbolic rather than a literal reproduction of his own dream life. Not only his familiarity with psychoanalytical material, but also his awareness of life and the work of other artists enabled him to reproduce imitations of dream states as, for example, Joyce was able to create imitations of the stream of consciousness. In these passages Miller is attempting to capture an emotion based on insight, an insight too fundamental, too obscure, too general for direct expression. The areas of his life which he most frequently expresses in these sequences are those involved with sexuality in its purest form, the very essence of sexual feeling which expands into the universe, until the universe itself becomes a great sexual orgy:

---

6. *Tropic of Capricorn,* 213.

Everything is packed into a second which is either consummated or not consummated. The earth is not an arid
plateau of health and comfort, but a great sprawling female
with velvet torso that swells and heaves with ocean billows;
she squirms beneath the diadem of sweat and anguish.
Naked and sexed she rolls among the clouds in the violet
light of the stars. All of her, from her generous breasts
to her gleaming thighs, blazes with furious ardor. She
moves among the seasons and the years with a grand
whoopla that seizes the torso with paroxysmal fury, that
shakes the cobwebs out of the sky; she subsides on her
pivotal orbits with volcanic tremors.[7]

Here the idea is relatively familiar, that of the fertility of
the universe, but the treatment is peculiarly Miller's. We feel that
we are relatively distanced from direct feeling. In other passages
both the idea and the treatment are further from usual human
experience; the imagery suggests direct penetration of the unconscious. In this passage Miller is dancing at a taxi-dance hall:

We taxi from one perfect female to another seeking the
vulnerable defect, but they are flawless and impermeable
in their impeccable lunar consistency. This is the icy white
maiden head of love's logic, the web of the ebbed tide, the
fringe of absolute vacuity. And on this fringe of the virginal logic of perfection I am dancing the soul dance of
white desperation, the last white man pulling the trigger
on the last emotion, the gorilla of despair beating his
breast with immaculate gloved paws. I am the gorilla who
feels his wings growing, a giddy gorilla in the center of a
satin-like emptiness; the night too grows like an electrical
plant, shooting white hot buds into velvet black space.
I am the black space of the night in which the buds break

7. *Tropic of Cancer*, 225-226.

with anguish, a starfish swimming on the frozen dew of the moon. I am the germ of a new insanity, a freak dressed in intelligible language, a sob that is buried like a splinter in the quick of the soul.[8]

The contrast in images here creates the emotion of the occasion, the contrast between the civilized and the primitive—"gorilla in immaculate gloved paws"—between hot and cold—"shooting white hot buds" with "icy white maiden head of love's logic." The situation which is supposed to be warm and passionate, supposed to stimulate erotic feeling, only induces a feverish search for lost emotions, frozen in the mechanistic world of the dance hall.

Since Miller uses fantasy as an important part of his total expression it is important whether it directly illuminates the world of unconscious association or symbolizes that world through the creation of a symbolic form. Although I believe that Miller as a writer has more than usual access to this world of unconscious elaboration, I believe even more strongly in the poetic quality of his imagination, and that his knowledge of dream symbolism led him to his particular style. That is not to say that these symbolic passages do not arise from material deeply perceived, but rather that he chose this form to express his own insights into unconscious states.

We have finally to examine Miller's cosmic consciousness as an element of his own experience. The feeling of being at one with the universe has been sought after since men have recorded their struggle with themselves and their environment. It has been called in recent psychological literature the "oceanic feeling." [9] To achieve this feeling is at once the most desired of human experiences and the most dangerous. The reason for the danger was not explicitly stated until the psychoanalytic investigations of this century revealed that the state of unconscious harmony which

---

8. *Tropic of Capricorn*, 121.
9. Otto Fenichel, *The Psychoanalytic Theory of Neurosis* (New York: W. W. Norton, 1945), 31ff.

characterizes the stage before birth could be sought so avidly that men would give up their life in reality. The desire for perfect security remains an aspect of all men's desires, but it remains also a threat, since regaining that security as it once existed would mean loss of self—or loss of consciousness, which is the same thing. Therefore the feeling of being at one with the cosmos must for the mature adult coexist with the fullest attainment of consciousness. It is upon this point that the successful journey into the self depends. When that journey awakens fears of the return of primordial darkness, unconscious life itself is experienced as something dark and threatening, like the dark world of "Christabl," or the caves of Hawthorne. On the other hand when the individual arrives at full acceptance of the self through the inward journey and discovers the world as a place of growth and development, then the stage is set for the experience of unity which is called cosmic consciousness.

Few of the Romantics claimed to have attained this state. Coleridge recognized the unconscious world as both the source of vital energy and as a threat. Hawthorne and Melville tended to fear the dark side. Wordsworth came closer, but his regressive orientation ultimately forced him to surrender in order to preserve full identity. By embracing the dichotomy of love and death in his transcendental poems, Whitman went further than the other Romantics in evoking the sense of cosmic consciousness. Miller is closest to Whitman in this regard. The movement toward cosmic consciousness must come through a death of the self. The descent to the womb, which awakens the terrors of loss of self, also enables the person to throw off his accumulated prejudices. Coming back, then, to reality, he goes through a series of "births," each of which brings him closer to his true self. To the fully developed person in his new state of awareness there comes too the expanded ability to love, by means of which he is able to break through the ego barriers, to feel at one with the universe. This was the meaning to Whitman's message of love; it is the main theme of Henry Miller. The search for unity never stops, but there are two ways to find it, by regression and progression. One cannot stop. One must be born every minute or give up and die.

Cosmic consciousness, the experience of unity, is the latest gift of the romantic idea to the modern world. More and more writers have adopted the view that the industrial world is a world of death, that men are, in fact, dying of ennui and restlessness. The Romantics foresaw the dangers which the trends of their time held; those dangers were reinterpreted by Whitman for his times. Miller has attempted to give them new form in our century. It is his great power that for many he can make the danger so real and the process of rebirth so compelling.

SELECTED CHECKLIST

Adams, Phoebe.
"Reader's Choice" (Review of *Big Sur and the Oranges of Hieronymus Bosch*), *Atlantic*, CC (August, 1957), p. 82.

Anon.
"An American in Paris" (A Review of Alfred Perles' *My Friend Henry Miller*), *Times Literary Supplement*, No. 2826 (April 27, 1956), p. 247.

Anon.
"Aphrodite Ascending," *Time*, Vol. 46, No. 26 (December 24, 1945), pp. 104, 106, 108. A review of *The Air-Conditioned Nightmare* by Miller, and *The Happy Rock* edited by Bern Porter.

Anon.
"(Article About Henry Miller)," *Davar Hashavu's*, No. 4 (January 24, 1957), pp. 10-11, 19.

Anon.
"Banned Books," *Books and Bookmen*, III, No. 11 (August, 1958), p. 3.

Anon.
"Big Sur Country," *Flair,* I (June, 1950), pp. 26-7.

Anon.
"Big Sur Realism," *Time,* Vol. 69, No. 23 (June 10, 1957), pp. 106-107. A review: *Big Sur and the Oranges of Hieronymus Bosch.*

Anon.
"Children . . . and Ourselves; Goodbye to Blue Yonder?" *Manas,* XXII, No. 35 (September 2, 1959), p. 5, 8.

Anon.
"Children . . . and Ourselves; Unnecessary Fears," *Manas,* XII, No. 33 (August 19, 1959), p. 5.

Anon.
"Dithyrambic Sex," *Time,* XXXII (November 21, 1938), p. 69.

Anon.
Facsimile of Henry Miller handwriting, pictures of him and his wife, water colors by Miller, and additions to Bibliography of Henry Miller's work since its publication in Appendix of *My Friend Henry Miller* by Alfred Perles, 1955, in *The Colorado Review,* Vol. III (Winter, 1958-1959), pp. 11-14, 24.

Anon.
"Henry Miller's Biblioteque Ideal" (Review of *The Books in My Life*), *Antiquarian Bookman,* X (November 1, 1952), p. 1198.

Anon.
"Henry Miller/Letters to Anaïs Nin," *Penthouse,* Vol. 1, No. 4 (August, 1965, London), pp. 11-14, 68-69.

Anon.
"Impressions of Burges," *Colorado Review,* I, No. 1 (Winter 1956-57), pp. 35-7.

Anon.

"Landscapes into Fish," *Time,* Vol. 49, No. 15 (April 14, 1947), p. 53. Comments on Miller's interest in watercolor painting.

Anon.

"Life by Mail Order," *Time,* Vol. 42, No. 24 (December 13, 1953), p. 55.

Anon.

"Miller," *Time,* XXXIV (December 25, 1939), pp. 54-55.

Anon.

"Miller, Henry" *Funk and Wagnalls Standard Reference Encyclopedia,* Vol. 17, New York, Standard Reference Works Publishing Company, 1959, p. 6076.

Anon.

New York Times (June 9, 1957), p. 22.

Anon.

"Passion and Prejudice" (Review of *Remember to Remember*), *Times Literary Supplement,* No. 2680 (June 12, 1953), p. 376.

Anon.

"Pentraits," Henry Miller, A Prodigal Grows in Brooklyn," *What's Doing,* I (June, 1946), pp. 13, 33-35.

Anon.

(Portrait), in *Aperature,* Vol. 7, No. 1 (1959), p. 31.

Anon.

(Review of *Big Sur and the Oranges of Hieronymus Bosch*), *New York Times Book Review* (June 9, 1957), p. 22.

Anon.

(Review of *Hamlet,* Vol. 2), *Experimental Review,* No. 3 (September, 1941) (unpaged).

Anon.

(Review of *Remember to Remember*), *The New Yorker*, Vol. 23 (November 8, 1947), p. 126.

Anon.

(Review of *Reunion in Barcelona*), *Trace*, Vol. 32 (June, July, 1959), pp. 30-31.

Anon.

(Review of *The Books in My Life*), *New York Times Book Review* (January 18, 1953), p. 3.

Anon.

(Review of *The Books in My Life*), *Times (London) Literary Supplement* (July 4, 1952), p. 434.

Anon.

(Review of *The Henry Miller Reader*, edited by Lawrence Durrell), *New York Times Book Review* (December 20, 1959), p. 10.

Anon.

(Review of *The Smile at the Foot of the Ladder*), *Kirkus*, Vol. 16 (June 1, 1948), p. 269.

Anon.

(Review of *The Time of the Assassins; a Study of Rimbaud*) *Times (London) Literary Supplement*, August 17, 1956), p. 482.

Anon.

(Review of *Tropic of Capricorn*), *Experimental Review*, No. 2 (November, 1940), pp. 78-80.

Anon.

"Reviews of Significant Journals," *Purpose*, Vol. X, No. 4 (October, December, 1938). Remarks concerning Henry Miller and his works are found on pages 238, 243, and 250.

Anon.

"Rugged, Romantic World Apart," *Life Magazine,* Vol. 47, No. 1 (July 6, 1959), pp. 56-63+.

Anon.

(Short Sketch of Miller's Life), *New Directions 16 in Prose and Poetry,* New York, New Directions, 1957, p. 262.

Anon.

"Sour Orange Juice," *Time,* Vol. 68, No. 7 (August 13, 1956), pp. 78-79. A review: *A Devil in Paradise.*

Anon.

"Special H. M. Number," *Synthesis* (Fevrier/Mars, Brussels, 1967).

Anon.

"Submissive and Sexless?" *Newsweek,* Vol. 50 (November 25, 1957), p. 119.

Anon.

The Henry Miller Literary Society. Upper Midwest Chapter, Minneapolis, Minnesota. "Historical Correspondence Involving Henry Miller" (loose). Correspondence dated September, 1957.
A. Letters from Trygve Hirsch, attorney of Oslo, Norway 2p.
  1. Enclosure from Peter P. Rohde, Denmark, 5p.
  2. Enclosure from Johan Voght, Norway (An excerpt or "Cut"—as the Norwegians would say—from his recent book. 7p.
B. Henry Miller's Letter in answer . . . mimeographed. 3 pp.

Anon.

"The International Henry Miller Letter," Nijmegan, Netherlands, Nos. 1-6 (June 1961-April 1964), ed. Henk van Gelre.

Anon.

"The Last Expatriate," in *Time,* Vol. 51, No. 26 (June 28, 1948), p. 92. A review: *The Smile at the Foot of the Ladder.*

Anon.

"The Mystic Cult of Sex and Necromancy, Report on What's Doing Around Little Sur and Peppermint by the Sea," *The California Pelican,* LIII (May, 1957), pp. 18-19.

Anon.

"The Object All Sublime" (Discussion of *Maurizius Forever*), *Manas,* X (May 8, 1957), pp. 1-2, 7-8.

Anon.

"The Tropic Myth" *(London) Times Literary Supplement,* 1 (November, 1963), p. 892.

Anon.

"Two Pal Joeys," *Time,* Vol. 67, No. 24 (June 11, 1956), pp. 114, 116. A review: *My Friend Henry Miller.*

Anon.

"What Do You Think?" (Letters from readers about Henry Miller articles), *Books and Bookmen,* V, No. 7 (April, 1960), p. 3.

Arbush, Art.

"Henry Miller's Erotica in Abstract," *Art and Photography,* Vol. 8, No. 7-91 (January, 1957), pp. 9-12, 46-47.

Armitage, Merle.

"The Man Behind the Smile," *Texas Quarterly,* IV, No. 4 (Winter, 1961-62), pp. 154-61.

Baker, Carlos.

"Mr. Miller's Garden of Eden," *New York Times Book Review* (June 9, 1957), p. 22.

Baker, Carlos.

(Review of *Big Sur and the Oranges . . .*), *New Yorker,* XXXIII (June 15, 1957), p. 127.

Bald, Wambly.
"La Vie de Boheme," *Chicago Tribune,* Paris edition (October 14, 1941).

Bard, Gene.
(Review of *Big Sur and the Oranges . . .*), *New York Herald Tribune Book Review* (August 18, 1957), p. 2.

Barker, George.
(Review of *Colossus of Maroussi or The Spirit of Greece*), *Nation,* Vol. 154 (January 3, 1942), p. 17.

Barrett, William.
"His Exuberant Reflections," in "Henry Miller: Man in Quest of Life," *Saturday Review,* XL (August 3, 1957), p. 8.

Batallie, Georges.
"La Morale De Miller," *Critique,* I (June, 1946), pp. 3-17.

Baxter, Annette Kar.
Henry Miller Expatriate, University of Pittsburgh Press, 1961.

Baxter, Annette Kar.
"Random Brushstrokes of a Radical Optimist," *New York Times Book Review* (July 8, 1962), pp. 6-7.

Bedford, Richard.
"Full of the Old Harry," *East-West Review,* II, 115-123.

Bedford, Richard C.
"The Apocatastasis of Henry Miller," *Dissertation Abstracts,* XXI (1960), 1560-61 (Iowa).

Bittencourt, Renato.
"Miller, Neurosis and Ecstasy," *Revista Branca,* No. 30 (1954), pp. 106-11.

Bittner, William.
"A Kind of Genius," *Nation,* Vol. 182 (May 26, 1956), pp. 455-456. Reviews: *The Time of the Assassins,* and *My Friend Henry Miller.*

Bittner, William.
(Review of *Time of the Assassins*), *Nation,* CLXXXII (May 26, 1956), p. 455.

Blocker, Gunter.
Die Neuen Wirklichkeiten Berlin, 1957.

Bluefarb, Sam.
"Have You Read? . . . Some Thoughts on Henry Miller," *Info-Mat,* I (December, 1952), p. 3.

Bradinsky, Oscar (ed.).
Of, By and About Henry Miller, Alicat Bookshop Press, Yonkers, New York, 1947.

Brady, Mildred Edie.
"The New Cult of Sex and Anarchy," *Harper Magazine,* Vol. 194 (April, 1947), pp. 312-322.

Breit, H.
"Big Sur," *New York Times Book Review* (March 11, 1956), p. 8.

Brown, Lionel.
"King of the Four-Lettered Words," *Modern Man,* VI (August, 1956), pp. 14, 18, 50-51.

Callaway, H. L.
"Henry Miller," in Steinbert, S. H. (ed.), *Cassell's Encyclopedia of World Literature,* Vol. II, New York, Funk and Wagnalls Co., 1953, p. 120.

Capouya, Emile.
"Henry Miller," *Salmagundi*, I, i, 81-87.

Carlbom, Arthur.
(Review of *Big Sur and the Oranges . . .*), *San Francisco Chronicle* (June 2, 1957), p. 23.

Cecil, Lord David.
"The Traveller Comes Home" (Review of *Big Sur*), *Times Literary Supplement* (May 2, 1958), p. 242.

Cendrars, Blaise.
(Reviews of *Tropic of Cancer*), *Orbes* (1935).

Chairmonte, Nicola.
"Return of Henry Miller," *New Republic*, Vol. III (December 4, 1944), pp. 751, 754. Includes a review of *Sunday After the War*.

Chisholm, Hugh.
"A Man Sized World. Letter to Henry Miller in Big Sur, California, from Hugh Chisholm in Athens, Greece," *Town and Country* (December, 1957) (pagination not determined).

Ciardi, John.
"Tropic of Cancer," *Saturday Review*, XLV, 26 (June 30, 1962), p. 13.

Cimatti, Pietro.
"L'inimitable Miller," *Fiera Letteraria*, XVII, xxi, 4, 6, 1961.

Clark, Eleanor.
"Images of Revolt," *Partisan Review*, VII (March-April, 1940), pp. 160-63.

Cockcroft, George P.
"The Two Henry Millers," *DA* 28:669A (Columbia).

Connolly, Cyril.
"(Review of *The Books in My Life*), *Sun Times* (May 18, 1952), p. 9.

Conroy, Jack.
(Review of *Sunday After the War*), *Book Week* (October 8, 1944), p. 9.

Corle, Edwin.
"About Henry Miller," *The Smile at the Foot of the Ladder*, Duell, Sloan, and Pearce, New York, 1948.

Cranaki, Mimica.
"Conversation with Henry Miller," *Greece*, London: Houlton, pp. 77-90.

Crandall, Steve.
"Henry Miller: Pornographer or Pioneer?" *Gallant*, I No. 1 (May, 1959), pp. 10-12.

D'Azevedo, Warren.
"Henry Miller and the Fifth Freedom, Reply to Open Letter," *New Republic*, Vol. 110 (February 14, 1944), pp. 212-213.

Delpech, Jeanine.
"L'enfer méne au paradis," *Nouvelles Littéraires*, 14 (May, 1958), pp. 1-2

Denat, Antonie.
"Henry Miller: Barocker Clown, Mystiker und Uberwinder. Zu seinem 70. Geburtstag." *Der Monat*, XIV No. 159, (1961), pp. 27-32.

den Haan, J.
"A Dream of a Book," *Kroniek Van Kunsten Kultur*, Amsterdam, Netherlands (December, 1949), 7 pp. A description of and information about the book *Into the Night Life*.

Desmond, Art.
"The Most Wonderful Rat," *Dale Harrison's Chicago,* I (July 5, 1958), p. 8.

Deutsch, Babette.
(Review of *Colossus of Maroussi* and *Wisdom of the Heart*), *Books* (January 11, 1942), p. 16.

Dewitt, G.
"Henry Miller's Unstitched Wound," *Blue Guitar,* No. 20 (Fall, 1962).

Dick, Kenneth C.
Henry Miller: Colossus of One, Sittard, Alberts, 1967.

Dillon, R. H.
Review of *Big Sur and the Oranges . . .,* *Library Journal,* LXXXII (July, 1957), p. 1770.

DuBois, Pierre H.
"Henry Miller en de mythe van het moment," *Een Houding in de Tijd;* essays. Amsterdam, J. M. Meulenhoff, 1950.

Durrell, Lawrence.
"Studies in Genius: Henry Miller," *Horizon,* Vol. 20 (July, 1949), pp. 45-61.

Durrell, Lawrence.
"The Shades of Dylan Thomas," *Encounter,* IX (December, 1957) pp. 56-9. (numerous mentions of Miller.)

Durrell, Lawrence, Alfred Perles, and Henry Miller.
Art and Outrage, E. P. Dutton and Co., New York, 1961.

Elliott, Desmond.
"The Ego of Henry Miller," (Books that Shocked—II), *Books and Bookmen* (March, 1960), p. 10.

Fadiman, Clifton.
(A Review of) *The Cosmological Eye, New Yorker,* XV (November 18, 1939), p. 105.

Fadiman, Clifton.
(A Review of *Wisdom of the Heart), New Yorker,* XVII (December 27, 1941), p. 60.

Fauchery, Pierre.
"Une Epopee du Sexe, le feuilleton bebdomadaire," *Action* (Paris), (April 1946).

Fiedler, Leslie A.
(Review of *The Books in My Life), Yale Review* XLII, No. 3 (Spring 1953), pp. 455-60.

Foster, Steven.
"A Critical Appraisal of Henry Miller's *Tropic of Cancer,*" *TCL,* IX, 196-208.

Fowlie, Wallace.
Age of Surrealism, Swallow Press, New York, 1950 (pp. 184-7 concerned with Miller).

Fowlie, Wallace.
(Review of *Big Sur and the Oranges . . .), Accent,* XVII (Summer 1957), pp. 188-92.

Fowlie, Wallace.
(Review of *The Time of the Assassins; a study of Rimbaud), New York Times Book Review* (March 4, 1956), p. 20.

Fowlie, Wallace.
"Shadow of Doom: an Essay on Henry Miller," *Accent* (Autumn, 1944), pp. 49-53.

Fraenkel, Michael.
Defense du Tropique du Cancer; Avec des Inedits de Miller,
Paris (June, 1957).

Fraenkel, Michael.
The Genesis of The Tropic of Cancer, Bern Porter, Berkeley,
California, 1946.

Freemantle, Anne.
"Expatriate's End," *Commonweal,* Vol. 47 (December 12, 1947),
pp. 229-230. Includes a review of *Remember to Remember.*

Friedman, Alan.
"The Pitching of Love's Mansion in the *Tropics* of Henry
Miller," *Seven Contemporary Authors,* ed. Thomas B. Whit-
bread, University of Texas Press, 1966.

Fukuzawa, Ichiro.
"Water Paintings of Henry Miller" translated by Shigeo Kitano
of Japanese text by Ichiro Fukuzawa from the art and literature
review *Gei jut-su-Shincho,* Tokyo (July, 1955), *The Colorado
Review,* Vol. III (Winter 1958-59), pp. 311-4.

Glicksberg, Charles I.
"A Milder Miller" (Review of *Remember to Remember*), *The
Southwest Review,* XXXIII (Summer 1948), pp. 311-14.

Glicksberg, Charles I.
"Henry Miller: Individualism in Extremis," *Southwest Review*
XXXIII (Summer 1948), pp. 289-95

Gold, Herbert.
"A Rotating Set of Messages From a Life-Loving Stoic," *New
York Times Book Review* (April 21, 1963), p. 5.

Goll, Yvan.
"Histoire de Parmenia L'Havanaise a Henry Miller," *Circle,*
Vol. 1, No. 3 (1944), p. 12.

Gordon, William A.
The Mind and Art of Henry Miller, Louisiana State University Press, 1968.

Gordon, William A.
Writer and Critic: A Correspondence with Henry Miller, Louisiana State University Press, 1968.

Gorlier, Claudio.
"La Retorica Del Proscritto," *Paragone* (November, 1958) pp. 63-77.

Grauer, Ben.
"Henry Miller: A First Audition of a Great American Writer," *Artesian, a Natural Flowing Well of Expression in the Arts,* Vol. 3, No. 3 (Summer 1958), pp. 12-13. Remarks of record "Henry Miller Recalls and Reflects," recorded in conversation with Ben Grauer, New York, April, 1956.

Granlid, Hans O.
"Friheten och Mardrommen: Henry Miller som Reseskildrare," *Studiekamraten,* 49 (1967), pp. 74-82.

Greer, Scot, *et. al.*
"To Be Or Not: 4 Opinions on Henry Miller's *The Smile At The Foot Of The Ladder,*" *The Tiger's Eye,* No. 5 (October 20, 1948), pp. 68-72.

Grenier, Roger.
"Henri Miller ou L'Obsession du Panthéisme," *Les Temps Modernes,* I Année, No. 8 (Mai, 1946), pp. 1527-33.

Guaraldi, Antonio.
"Individual e societa in Henry Miller," *Aut. Aut,* No. 78-80, pp. 98-114.

Haan, Jacques Den.
Milleriana, Vitgeverij de Bexige Bij, Amsterdam.

Haggqvist, Arne.
Obehagliga Forfattare, Ars Forlag, Stockholm, 1953.

Halsband, Robert.
(Review of *The Time of the Assassins* and *My Friend Henry Miller*), *Saturday Review,* Vol. 39 (May 5, 1956), pp. 15ff.

Hassan, Ihab.
"The Literature of Silence: From Henry Miller to Beckett and Burroughs," *Encounter,* 28, i (1967), pp. 74-82.

Hassan, Ihab.
The Literature of Silence: Henry Miller and Samuel Beckett, New York, 1968.

Haverstick, Hohn, and William Barrett.
"Henry Miller: Man in Quest of Life," *Saturday Review,* Vol. 40, No. 31 (August 3, 1957), pp. 8-10.

Hirsch, Trygve.
(Introduction to Miller's "Defense of the Freedom to Read"), *Evergreen Review,* Vol. 3, No. 9 (Summer 1959), p. 12.

Hoffman, Frederick J.
"Further Interpretations," *Freudianism and the Literary Mind,* Louisiana State University Press, 1945, pp. 277-308.

Hoffman, Frederick J.
"Henry Miller, Defender of the Marginal Life," *The Thirties: Fiction, Poetry, Drama,* ed. Warren French, Deland, Florida (1967).

Holmes, Blanca.
"Henry Miller and Clifford Odets," *American Astrology,* XXV (July 1957), pp. 29-31.

Hughs, Warren.
"The Soul of Anaesthesia" (Review of *Air-Conditioned Nightmare*), Index, I (March, 1946), pp. 2-6.

Hutchison, Earl R., Sr.,
"Henry Miller and *Tropic of Cancer:* From Paris to Wisconsin On the Censorship Trail," *DA,* 28 (1967), 1389-a-85a (Wisc.).

Huxley, Aldous.
"Death and the Baroque," *Harper's,* CXCVIII (April, 1949), pp. 80-6.

Jackson, J. H.
(Review of *The Smile at the Foot of the Ladder*), *San Francisco Chronicle* (June 28, 1948), p. 16.

Jackson, Paul R.
"Henry Miller: The Autobiographical Romances," *DA,* 28:678A (Columbia).

James, Edith
(Review of *Remember to Remember*), *San Francisco Chronicle* (December 4, 1947), p. 16.

Jonsson, Thorsten.
Sider av Amerika, Albert Bonniers, Stockholm, 1946.

Kahn, Albert E.
"Odyssey of a Stool Pigeon," *New Currents,* III, No. 3-4 (January, 1945), p. 26.

Kaplan, H. J.
(A Review of *The Colossus of Maroussi*), *Partisan Review,* IX (January-February, 1942), pp. 85-86.

Katz, Joseph.
"Henry Miller's *Beauford Delaney:* A Correction," *AN&Q,* 5:68.

Kazin, Alfred.
On Native Grounds, Harcourt, Brace and Co., New York, 1942.

Kees, Weldon.
"Unhappy Expatriate," *New York Times Book Review* (November 30, 1947), pp. 5, 45. Also (Review of *Remember to Remember*.)

Kennedy, Lou.
"Of Cabbages and Kings: Henry Miller and Sweeney the Rat," *This Week in Chicago* (July 2, 1949), pp. 16-17.

Kermode, Frank.
"Henry Miller and John Betjeman," *Puzzles and Epiphanies: Essays and Reviews, 1958-1961*, Chilmark Press, London, 1963.

King, Robin.
"Potted Miller" (Review of *Murder the Murderer* and *Sunday After The War*), *The New Statesman and Nation*, XXXIII (February 1, 1947), pp. 100-1.

Kleine, Don.
"Innocence Forbidden: Henry Miller in the Tropics," *Prairie Schooner*, XXXIII, No. 2 (Summer 1959), pp. 125-30.

Krim, Seymour.
"The Netherworld of Henry Miller," *Commonweal*, LVII (October 24, 1952), pp. 68-71.

Kronhausen, Phyllis and Eberhardt.
Pornography and the Law, Ballantine Books, New York, 1959.

Kunitz, Stanley Jasspon (ed.),
Twentieth Century Authors; 1st Supplement, H. W. Wilson Co., New York, 1955, pp. 670-71.

Kunitz, Stanley J., and Howard Haycraft (eds.),
Twentieth Century Authors—A Biographical Dictionary of Modern Literature, H. W. Wilson Co., New York, 1942, pp. 960-961.

Lee, Alwyn.
"Henry Miller—The Pathology of Isolation," *New World Writing*, No. 2, New York, 1952.

Legg, Morley D.
"Perceptions of a Creative Writer: An Introduction to Henry Miller," *Orgonomic Functionalism*, V (March 1958), pp. 91-102.

Leite, George.
"The Autochoton," *Angry Penguins*, 1945, pp. 137-140.

Leite, George.
"To Henry Miller," *Circle*, Vol. 1, No. 2 (1944) (p. 33; the magazine is unpaged).

Leonard, John.
"Henry Miller and the Spoiled Priests," *Root and Branch*, No. 2 (1962), pp. 77-80.

Lingel, Fred.
"Oh Me Oh Mighty: A Word To Hungry Artists," *The Leaves Fall*, III (January 1945), pp. 94-6 (a reply to Henry Miller's "What Are We Going to Do About Alf?").

Littlejohn, David.
"The Tropics of Miller," *New Republic*, CXLVI (March 5, 1962), pp. 31-5.

Lord, Russell.
"Henry Miller," *The Harvard Wake*, I (June 1945), pp. 13-16.

Lowenfels, Walter.
"Unpublished Preface to *Tropic of Cancer*," *Massachusetts Review*, V, 481-491.

Lund, Mary G.
"Henry Miller: A Fierce Oracle," *North Amer, Rev.* 4, i: 18-21.

Lundkvist, Arthur.
"Henry Miller och myten om den skapande doden," *Ikarus Flykt*, Albert Bonniers, Stockholm, 1939.

Lupi, Valeria.
"Henry Miller e l'America," *Nuova antologia*, XCVII, fasc. (1943), pp. 353-362.

Luzi, Mario.
Aspetti Della Generazione Napoleanica Ed Altri Saggi Di Letteratura Francese, Guonda Parma, 1956.

Macdonald, Dwight.
"Words Without End" (Review of *The Books In My Life*), *New York Times Book Review* (January 18, 1953), p. 3.

MacInnes, Colin.
"Benevolent Faun," *The Spectator* (April 5, 1963), p. 437.

Maine, Harold.
"Henry Miller: Bigotry's Whipping Boy," *Arizona Quarterly*, VII (Autumn 1951), pp. 197-208.

Manning, Hugo.
"Apropos Henry Miller," *The Wind and The Rain*, II (Winter 1945), pp. 166-8.

Marcuse, Ludwig.
"Miller, Henry," *Obscene: The History of an Indignation*, Tr. Karen Greshon, London, 1964.

Marshall, Margaret.
"Notes By The Way," *Nation*, Vol. 159 (November 4, 1944), p. 562. Includes a review of *Sunday After The War*.

Marshall, Margaret.
(Review of *Sunday After The War*), *Nation*, CLIX (November 4, 1944), p. 562.

Mauriac, Claude.
The New Literature (Tr. by Samuel I. Stone) C. Braziller, New York, 1959.

Mayoux, Jean-Jacques.
"De meilleur en Miller," *Etudes Anglaises,* XVI (1963), pp. 369-373. (Rev. Art.)

Mead, William
(Review of *The Air-Conditioned Nightmare*), *Briarcliff Quarterly,* III (July 1946), pp. 148-9.

Miller, *et. al.*
Of-By-And About Henry Miller, Alicat Bookshop Press, Yonkers, New York, 1947.

Mitchell, Edward Bell.
"Henry Miller: The Artist as Seer," *DA,* XXVI, 1047 (Conn.).

Mohn, Bent.
"Henry Miller's Sex-og Dods-dans," (sic) (Review of *Tropic of Capricorn*), *Information* (March 25, 1955), p. 4.

Moon, Eric.
"Too Hot to Handle," *Books and Bookmen,* III (April, 1958), p. 25.

Moore, Bob.
"A Note on Henry Miller," *Alumnus,* St. John's School, III, (1958), p. 1.

Moore, Everett T.
"*Tropic of Cancer:* The First Three Months," *Bulletin of the American Library Association,* LV (1961), pp. 779-80.

Moore, Harry T.
"Portrait Gallery and Pet Gripes," *Saturday Review,* XLV, 26, (June 30, 1962), p. 18.

Moore, Harry T.
(Review of *The Books In My Life*), *New York Times Book Review* (January 18, 1953), p. 3.

Moore, Nicholas.
Henry Miller, The Opus Press, Woodhouse, Cholesbury Road, Wigginton, Herts (England), 1943.

Moore, Thomas H. (ed.).
Bibliography of Henry Miller, Henry Miller Literary Society, Minneapolis, 1961.

Moravia, Alberto.
"Two American Writers," *Sewanee Review*, LXCIII (1960), pp. 473-81.

Muir, Edwin.
The Present Age from 1914, The Cresset Press, London, 1939. (Half Title: *Introduction to English Literature*, edited by Bonamy Dobree, Vol. V.)

Muller, Herbert.
"The World of Henry Miller," *Kenyon Review*, II (Summer 1940), pp. 312-18.

Neiman, Gilbert.
"No Rubbish, No Albatrosses: Henry Miller," *Rocky Mountain Review*, IX (Winter 1945), pp. 69-76.

Neiman, Gilbert.
(Review of *Big Sur and the Oranges* . . .), *New Mexico Quarterly*, XXVII, No. 1-2 (Spring-Summer, 1957), pp. 138-9.

Nelson, Jane A.
"Form and Image in The Fiction of Henry Miller," *DA*, 28 (1967): 2256a (Mich.).

Nelson, Jane A.
Form and Image in the Fiction of Henry Miller, New York, 1970.

Newton, Douglas.
"A Note on Henry Miller," *New English Weekly,* XXX (December 19, 1946) (pagination not determined).

Nin, Anaïs.
Preface to *Tropic of Cancer,* Obelisk Press, Paris (1950).

Nin, Anaïs.
Preface to *Tropic of Cancer,* with introduction by Lawrence R. Maxwell. Printed separately. March 15, 1947.

Omarr, Sydney.
"A Collection of Henry Miller" (Review of *The Henry Miller Reader*), *Los Angeles Times* (January 4, 1960) (pagination not determined).

Omarr, Sydney.
Henry Miller: His World of Urania, Villiers Pubs., London (1960). (An astrologer's view of his work; foreword by Henry Miller.)

Omarr, Sydney.
"Henry Miller Today," *Frontier,* VII (February, 1956), pp. 20-21.

Ormsby, Robert L.
"From the Faculty Scrapbooks," *The Berea Alumnus,* XVI (April, 1946), pp. 203-4, 206.

Orwell, George.
"Inside the Whale" (Excerpts by James Laughlin, ed.), *New Directions in Prose and Poetry,* Norfolk, Connecticut, 1940; *New Directions* (1940), pp. 205-246.

Orwell, George.
"Inside the Whale," *Such Were the Joys,* Gollancz, London, 1940; also Harcourt, Brace and Co., New York, 1953, pp. 154-199.

Parkinson, Thomas.
"The Hilarity of Henry Miller," *The Listener,* LIX, No. 1525 (June 19, 1958), pp. 1021-2.

Paulding, C. G.
(Review of *Sunday After the War*) *Commonweal,* Vol. 4 (January 5, 1945), p. 306.

Peignot, Jerome.
"Henry Miller ou le Juif manque," *Nouvelle Revue Française,* XII, 516-525.

Peltzer, Karl.
Das Treffende Zitat, Ott, Thun, 1957.

Perles, Alfred.
"Additions to Bibliography of Henry Miller's Work Since its Publication in Appendix of *My Friend Henry Miller,*" *Colorado Review,* III (Winter 1958-9), p. 14.

Perles, Alfred.
"Henry Miller in Villa Seurat; an Incomplete Portrait," *Life and Letters Today* (England), Vol. 41 (June 1944), pp. 148-56.

Perles, Alfred.
"I Live on My Wits," *Horizon,* I (July, 1940), pp. 504-22.

Perles, Alfred.
"Letters to Henry Miller," *Horizon,* II (December, 1940), pp. 290-9.

Perles, Alfred.
My Friend Henry Miller, Longmans, Toronto, Canada, 1956.

Perles, Alfred.
Reunion in Big Sur; a letter to Henry Miller in reply to his reunion in Barcelona. Scorpion Press, Northwood, Middlesex, 1959.

Perles, Alfred, and Lawrence Durrell.
Art and Outrage: A Correspondence about Henry Miller Between Alfred Perles and Lawrence Durrell (with an intermission by Henry Miller). Putnam and Co. Ltd., London, 1959. "Works by Henry Miller," pp. 62-3. Also printed by E. P. Dutton Co., New York, 1961.

Perles, Alfred, and Neville Spearman.
My Friend Henry Miller, John Day Co., New York, 1956.

Politis, M. J.
"In Understanding of Greece" (Review of *The Colossus of Maroussi*), *New York Times Book Review* (March 29, 1942), p. 24.

Poore, Charles.
"Henry Miller Sets Down a Tanbark Parable," *New York Times Book Review* (June 6, 1948), p. 6. A review of *The Smile At The Foot Of The Ladder.*

Porter, Bern (ed.).
Happy Rock: A Book about Henry Miller. Bern Porter, Berkeley, California, 1945.

Porter, Bern.
Henry Miller, A Chronology and Bibliography. Bern Porter, Berkeley, California, 1945, Incomplete.

Powell, Larry.
"Argument about Astrology," *Manas,* IX (September 5, 1956), pp. 6-7.

Powell, Lawrence Clark.
Books in My Baggage, World Publishing Co., Cleveland, 1960 (a reprint of the author's introduction to *The Intimate Henry Miller*).

Powell, Lawrence Clark.
"Miller of Big Sur," *Books in My Baggage,* World Publishing Co., Cleveland, 1960, pp. 148, 53.

Powell, Lawrence Clark.
"We Moderns," *Scop,* I (Summer 1945), pp. 5-6.

Queval, Jean.
"Henry Miller," *Poesie,* 47, No. 37, 1947, pp. 110-14.

Rahv, Philip.
"The Artist as Desperado," *New Republic,* Vol. 104 (April 21, 1941), pp. 557-59.

Rahv, Philip.
"Henry Miller," *Image and Idea,* New Directions, New York, 1949, pp. 144-50.

Rahv, Philip (ed.).
"Miller, Henry. Vive la France," *Discovery of Europe: the Story of American Experience in the Old World . . .,* Houghton Mifflin, Co., Boston, 1947, pp. 205-46.

Rahv, Philip.
"Spellbinder in Greece" (Review of *Colossus of Maroussi and Wisdom of the Heart*), *New Republic,* Vol. 106 (January 12, 1942), pp. 59-60.

Read, Herbert.
"As the Grass Grows" (Review of *Big Sur . . .*), *New Statesman,* LV (March 29, 1958), p. 410.

Read, Herbert Edward.
"Henry Miller," in Sir Herbert Read (ed.), *The Tenth Muse: Essays in Criticism*, Routledge and Kegan Paul, London, 1957, pp. 250-55.

Read, Herbert.
"Views and Reviews: Henry Miller" (Review of *Sunday After The War*) *New English Weekly* (London) (December 28, 1944)

Read, Herbert.
What England's Leading Critic Thinks About America's Most Extraordinary Writer—Herbert Read on Henry Miller (pamphlet reprinted from *The New English Weekly*), (1946), New York.

Renken, Maxine.
"Bibliography of Henry Miller; 1945-61," *Twentieth Century Literature*, VII, pp. 180-90.

Rexroth, Kenneth.
"The Neglected Henry Miller," *Nation*, Vol. 181, No. 19 (November 5, 1955), pp. 385-87.

Rexroth, Kenneth.
"Reality of Henry Miller," *Bird in the Bush, Obvious Essays*, New York, 1959, pp. 154-67.

Riley, Esta Lou.
Henry Miller: An Informal Bibliography, 1924-60, Fort Hayes Studies, New Series, Bibliog. Ser., No. 1, Fort Hayes Kansas State College, Hays, Kansas.

Ritter, Paul.
"Book Reviews: *Big Sur* . . . ," *Orgonomic Functionalism*, V (March, 1958), pp. 127-31.

Robischon, Thomas.
"A Day In Court With The Literary Critic," *Massachusetts*

Review, (University of Massachusetts), VI (1964065), pp. 101-110. (*On Tropic of Cancer,* especially.)

Rode, Alex.
"Henry Miller: The Novelist as Liberator," *Americas,* XVIII, 41-43.

Rose, Edward J.
"The Aesthetics of Civil Disobedience: Henry Miller, Twentieth Century Transcendentalist," *Edge* (Edmonton, Can.), I, i (Autumn 1963).

Rosenfeld, Paul.
"Hamlet is Not Enough," *Nation,* CLI (September 7, 1940), p. 198.

Rosenfeld, Paul.
"The Traditions and Henry Miller," *The Nation,* Vol. 149, No. 19 (November 4, 1939), pp. 502-503. (A review of *Tropic of Capricorn.*)

Rosenfeld, Paul.
"We Want Fortinbras," *Nation,* CLIII (August 16, 1941), p. 146.

Rosenthal, M. L.
"The Millennium of Henry Miller" (A review of *Big Sur and the Oranges of Hieronymous Bosch*), *Nation,* Vol. 184, No. 23 (June 8, 1957), pp. 502-3.

Roth, Samuel.
"An Open Letter to Henry Miller," *American Aphrodite: A Quarterly for the Fancy Free,* IV, No. 14 (1954), pp. 3-4.

Russell, Sanders.
"The Golden Heresy," *Contour Quarterly,* No. 2 (September 1947), pp. 26-30.

Sandall, Tom.
"Henry Miller's Universum," *Nya Argus*, LVII (1964), pp. 242-244.

Sanquineti, Edorado.
"Henry Miller, una poetica barocca," *Verri*, VI (1962), i, pp. 26-39.

Schmiele, Walter.
Henry Miller in Selbstzeugnissen und Bildokumenten, Rowohly, Hamburg, 1961.

Schneider, Duane (ed.).
Unpublished Letters From The Diary of Anaïs Nin, Duane Schneider Press, Inc., Athens, Ohio, 1968.

Shapiro, Harvey.
Review of "New Directions 9," *Yale Poetry Review*, II (Summer 1946), pp. 31-2. (Miller had an essay on Rimbaud in this.)

Shapiro, Karl.
"Greatest Living Author," *In Defense of Ignorance*, New York: Random House, pp. 313-38, 1960. (Originally published in *Two Cities*, December, 1959).

Sherman, Stuart C.
"Defending the Freedom to Read: A Case History of Resistance to Censorship and Conformity," *Library Journal*, LXXXVII, pp. 479-83. (The "case" is *Tropic of Cancer*, 1962.)

Shorey, Katherine.
(Review of *Air Conditioned Nightmare*), *Library Journal*, Vol. 70, No. 21 (December 1, 1945), p. 1134.

Smith, J.
"I am an Artist: an Editorial," *Saturday Review*, Vol. 40 (August 3, 1957), p. 18.

Smith, Harrison.
"The New Coast of Bohemia," *Saturday Review,* XXX (August 18, 1947).

Smithline, Arnold.
"Henry Miller and the Transcendental Spirit," *Emerson Society Quarterly,* No. 43, pp. 50-6.

Soroyan, Chesley.
"The Rosey Crucifixion: A Review," *Points,* No. 4 (October-November, 1949), pp. 79-83.

Southern, Terry.
"Miller: Only the Beginning," *Nation,* CXCIII (November 18, 1961), p. 399.

Spender, Stephen.
"Tour West—Some Random Notes," *Kirkeby Hotels Magazine,* V (February 1949), pp. 9-11, 61-3.

Stuhlmann, Gunther.
Henry Miller: Letters to Anaïs Nin, G. P. Putnam's Sons, 1965.

Sutton, Denys.
"The Challenge of American Art," *Horizon,* XX (October, 1949), pp. 268-284.

Sykes, Gerald.
"The Postman Rings Twice," *New York Times Book Review* (April 14, 1963), p. 16.

Theobald, John.
Review of "New Directions 9," *The New Mexico Quarterly Review,* XVI (Autumn 1946), pp. 365-9.

Thompson, Dunston.
"Little Boy Blue" (Review of *The Cosmological Eye*), *New Republic,* CII (January 8, 1940), p. 61.

Traschen, Isador.
"Henry Miller: The Ego and I," *South Atlantic Quarterly*, LXV, 345-354.

Ustvedt, Ynguar.
"Introduksjon Til Henry Miller," *Samtiden*, LXXI, 297-305.

Venetikos, Alexandros.
"Letters from Phaestos [to Henry Miller]," *Wanderlust*, I, No. 4 (January, 1959), pp. 20-1.

Villa, Georges.
Miller et l'amour, Correa, Paris, 1947.

Wallbridge, Earl F.
(Review of "The Books in My Life"), *Library Journal*, Vol. 77, No. 17 (October 1, 1952), p. 1650.

Warfel, Harry R.
"Henry Miller," *American Novelists of Today*, American Book Co., New York, 1951, p. 304.

Weiss, T.
"Kenneth Patchen and Chaos as Vision," *Briarcliff Quarterly*, III (July 1946), pp. 127-34. (Compares Patchen and Miller).

West, Herbert Faulkner.
"Camerado," *Dartmouth Alumni Magazine*, Vol. 29 (1937), pp. 9, 72.

West, Herbert Faulkner.
"The Strange Case of Henry Miller," *The Mind on The Wing: a Book for Readers and Collectors*. Coward-McCann, Inc., 1947, pp. 115-38.

Westerlinck, Albert.
"Henry Miller," *DWB*, cvii, 519-520.

Wheeler, Dinsmore.
(Review of *Air-Conditioned Nightmare*), *New Mexico Quarterly*, XVI, No. 4 (Winter 1946), pp. 510-1.

White, Emil.
Henry Miller—Between Heaven and Hell, Emil White, Big Sur, California, (1961).

Wickes, George.
"The Art of Fiction XXCIII, Henry Miller," *Paris Review*, 28 (Summer-Fall 1962), pp. 129-59. (Interview with Miller.)

Wickes, George.
Henry Miller. (Pamphlets on American Writers, 56.) University of Minnesota Press, Minneapolis.

Wickes, George (ed.).
Henry Miller and the Critics, Southern Illinois University Press Carbondale, Illinois, 1964.

Wickes, George.
"Henry Miller At Seventy," *Clairmont Quarterly*, Clairmont, California, IX, ii (1962), pp. 5-20.

Wickes, George (ed.).
Lawrence Durrell and Henry Miller: A Private Correspondence, E. P. Dutton, New York, 1964.

Widmer, Kingsley.
Henry Miller, Twayne Publishers, New York, 1963.

Williams, John.
"Henry Miller: The Success of Failure," *Virginia Quarterly Review* (Spring, 1968).

Williams, William Carlos.
"To The Dean," *Circle*, Vol. L, No. 2 (1944), p. 32.

Williams, William Carlos.
"To The Dean" (A Poem), in James McLaughlin (ed.), *New Directions 16 in Prose and Poetry*, New Directions, New York, 1957, p. 40.

Willis, Stanley.
"About California," *Right Angle*, II (December, 1948), pp. 4-5.

Wilson, Edmund.
(Review of "The Air Conditioned Nightmare)," *New Yorker*, XXI (December 29, 1945), pp. 54-8.

Wilson, Edmund.
(Review of *Sunday After the War*), *New Yorker*, XX (October 21, 1944), pp. 87-91.

Wilson, Edmund.
"Twilight of the Expatriates," *Shores of Light; a Literary Chronicle of the Twenties and Thirties*. Farrar, Straus & Giroux, New York, 1952, pp. 705-10.

Wood, Richard C. (ed.).
Collector's Quest: The Correspondence of Henry Miller and J. Rives Child, 1947-1965. University of Virginia Press, Charlottesville.

Wylie, Philip.
"Run for your Lives" (A Review of *The Air-Conditioned Nightmare*), *Saturday Review of Literature*, Vol. 29 (February 16, 1946), pp. 20-2.

Yalovlev, L.
"Literature of Decay," *Soviet Literature*, No. 6 (1950), pp. 172-178.

Yerbury, Grace D.
"Of A City Beside a River: Whitman, Eliot, Thomas, Miller," *Walt Whitman Review*, X, pp. 67-73.